The Man
with the
Baguette

Wanderings in Paris and Provence

JOHN BLATTNER

EAU CLAIRE BOOKS

The Man with the Baguette:
Wanderings in Paris and Provence

Copyright © John Blattner (2019)

All rights reserved. No part of this book may be reproduced, stored in a retrieval system, or transmitted, in any form or by any means, without the prior written permission of the publisher.

ISBN 978-1-7343075-0-4

EAU CLAIRE BOOKS
an imprint of WordCraft LLC

Photographs by John and Peggy Blattner
www.WordCraftLLC.com

Cover and interior design by Graphikitchen, L.L.C.
www.graphikitchen.com

To Peggy

La femme de ma vie

Contents

PROLOGUE	The Man with the Baguette	7
THURSDAY, MAY 2	*Nous Sommes Arrivés à Paris!*	11
FRIDAY, MAY 3	Exploring the Neighborhood	15
SATURDAY, MAY 4	La Marée Verte	19
SUNDAY, MAY 5	Ina Garten and the Burghers	23
MONDAY, MAY 6	Water Lilies, Bistros, and Brasseries	27
TUESDAY, MAY 7	Orsay and La Dernière Goutte	31
WEDNESDAY, MAY 8	Versailles	35
THURSDAY, MAY 9	The Umbrellas of Paris	39
FRIDAY, MAY 10	Picasso and The Bald Soprano	41
SATURDAY, MAY 11	*Anniversaire de Mariage*	45
SUNDAY, MAY 12	Saint-Germain-des-Près and the Marais	49
Paris Apartment		53
MONDAY, MAY 13	*Flâneurs*	57
TUESDAY, MAY 14	Rue Cler and Beyond	63
WEDNESDAY, MAY 15	Montmartre	67
THURSDAY, MAY 16	The Seine, the Panthéon, and Le Christine	71
FRIDAY, MAY 17	*Au Revoir à Paris*	75
Final Reflections on Paris		79
SATURDAY, MAY 18	On to Provence	83
SUNDAY, MAY 19	Market Day	87
MONDAY, MAY 20	The Antiques Village	91

TUESDAY, MAY 21	On the Road: Roussillon and Gordes	95
WEDNESDAY, MAY 22	*Jouets, Poupées*, and a Change in Plans	101
THURSDAY, MAY 23	Road Trip: Ménerbes and Lacoste	105
FRIDAY, MAY 24	*Terroirs* of the Rhône	111
SATURDAY, MAY 25	Le Prévôté	117
SUNDAY, MAY 26	Leonard	121
MONDAY, MAY 27	Arles, Les Baux, and St-Rémy	125
TUESDAY, MAY 28	Fontaine-de-Vaucluse	129
WEDNESDAY, MAY 29	Avignon: the Palace and the Bridge	131
THURSDAY, MAY 30	The Other Market Day	135
FRIDAY, MAY 31	Mont Ventoux, Wines of the Côtes du Rhône	139
SATURDAY, JUNE 1	Return to Ménerbes	145
SUNDAY, JUNE 2	Café Fleurs	149
MONDAY, JUNE 3	Homeward Bound, Day 1	151
TUESDAY, JUNE 4	Homeward Bound, Day 2	155
Epilogue		157

The Maubert-Mutualité Metro stop, where John first encountered the man with the baguette

PROLOGUE

The Man with the Baguette

In April 2003 my wife Peggy and I made a five-day visit to Paris. It was a whirlwind tour of major sites, museums, and monuments, and we loved every minute of it. One evening as we were walking from the Metro station to our hotel a man scurried by, wearing a small backpack and holding a sack with a baguette in it. I fancied that he was an honest-to-goodness *Parisien*, not a tourist, headed home at the end of the day with bread for the dinner table. Wouldn't it be great, I thought, to *be* that guy? To actually *live* in Paris? Just for a while? Long-term relocation wasn't in the cards, and even a year seemed out of reach. But how about a month? *Live a month in Paris.* It sounded good.

The thought stayed alive for years. More and more, as time went by, we began kicking around the idea of adding a sojourn in the south of France. Ultimately the vision morphed into "live in France for a month," split between Paris and, well, "the south of France." We settled on the month of May because it seemed ideal in terms of climate and avoiding the big summer crowds. In addition, it would be our 45th wedding anniversary. Where better to celebrate than Paris?

I started planning the trip several months in advance. For me, preparation and anticipation are key elements of any experience, and I threw myself into whole-heartedly.

The first step was figuring out where to stay in Paris. This was challenging. There are thousands of houses, condos, and apartments for rent in Paris. They all look and sound wonderful online. But who knows which are legit? As it happened, I discovered that my colleague Steve had visited the city many times and had found a rental agency that he liked. We found several attractive options on their website and settled on a two-bedroom apartment in a not-too-touristy part of Saint-Germain-des-Prés, in the 6th *Arrondissement* (Administrative District).

The next step was to nail down precisely what we meant by "the south of France." Aside from knowing that wine had to be involved, we had no idea where to begin. But once again serendipity rode to the rescue: our niece's mother-in-law, Myrna, is a part-time travel agent. She had once spent two weeks in a cozy apartment in the Provençal village of Isle-sur-la-Sorgue, not far from where the British writer Peter Mayle spent his storied *Year in Provence*. Myrna said she had loved the spot so much that "they had to drag me out." Endorsements like that don't come along every day, and we weren't about to argue with this one. We booked that very apartment.

Figuring out what to actually *do* in France was less of a challenge. Paris is inexhaustible, and even a small portion of Provence presents a multitude of opportunities. We've read a lot of books and done a lot of research, but we've resisted the temptation to make too many specific plans or reservations. The idea is simply to *be* in Paris and Provence, explore them at our leisure, soak up the local life and color. Just wandering the streets of Paris, finding "our" cafés and restaurants, strolling along the Seine, and later the Sorgue, has far more appeal than frantically checking museums, monuments, and cathedrals off a must-do list. We undoubtedly will do many of those things, though we don't feel any need to repeat some of the traditional items (Eiffel Tower, Mona Lisa, hop-on-hop-off bus) that we covered sixteen years ago.

A big part of the preparation has been recovering at least some facility with the French language. I took two years of French in junior high, four years in high school, and one semester in college—and have done absolutely nothing with it in the forty-plus years since. But it is amazing how much of it comes back: it's all etched onto the mental hard drive somewhere. It's fair to say that relearning French has been my main hobby since I retired from my law practice at the beginning of the year. I began by dabbling with Babbel, and Peggy and I took a private lesson from a local college prof. But both activities felt constricting. I've focused mainly on listening to podcasts; reading French books, stories, and online newspapers; and participating in a weekly conversation group, which has arguably been the most effective learning tool and certainly the most fun. I'm light years away from being fluent, or even proficient. But I dare to hope that I'll be able to get around in France without endangering or embarrassing myself too much. I'm told the French are appreciative when Americans make even feeble efforts to use their language. *On verra bien*!

• • •

Earlier I mentioned that preparing for and anticipating an experience is key to my enjoyment of it. So is recording and reliving it. Peggy and I have always kept short diaries of our trips, for the sake of helping us remember not only the high points but also the smaller details—the restaurants we liked, the people we met, what our hotels were like, what we'd do differently next time, and so on. This time I decided to keep a more comprehensive journal. I spent time every day tapping away on my iPad, recording not only the sights and sounds and tastes and adventures, but also how I felt about them and what I learned from them. I look forward to re-reading it in years to come, and to reliving the many wonderful experiences it records. And I'm happy to share it you.

The view from our apartment upon arrival

THURSDAY, MAY 2

Nous Sommes Arrivés à Paris!

The overnight flight from Detroit was smooth and navigation of Charles DeGaulle airport (CDG) was painless. I had read that it could take an hour or more to clear the border control checkpoint, and the massive Disney World-style queue labyrinth made it clear that CDG is indeed equipped to process many thousands of jet-lagged travelers. But today it was nearly empty. Our luggage arrived promptly and before we knew it we were in a taxi headed for *centre ville*.

Our apartment is located on Rue Princesse, a short, narrow street just a couple blocks off Boulevard Saint-Germain, the main thoroughfare in the district. It's a cozy two-bedroom on the *premier étage* (second storey), with contemporary styling that preserves exposed stone pillars and wooden beams. One intriguing feature is the number of books: shelves and shelves of them, including large collections of well-known English-language works translated into French: everything from my favorite novel, Richard Russo's *Nobody's Fool* (*"Un homme presque parfait"*), to Churchill's 12-volume history of World War II. It's a congenial environment for book lovers like us.

The property management is first-rate. We were greeted by a young lady from the agency who showed us around the apartment. She told us they had learned that the city planned an unspecified "public works" project on the street this week, and had made a 25 percent reduction in our rent to compensate for any inconvenience, with the promise of finding us alternative accommodations if noise became a problem. The project appears to be modest, but the agency's consideration and attention to detail was most welcome.

We were settled in by 1:00pm Paris time (which was 7:00am on our body clocks but felt like 11:00pm after a mostly sleepless red-eye flight) and took our first stroll around the neighborhood. It was chilly and drizzly but we didn't mind. The main destination was a local supermarket, Carrefour, where we bought milk, coffee, cheese, wine, and a few other items. We'll get more adventurous with the numerous *boulangeries, pâtisseries, charcuteries,* and other specialty markets in the area, but Carrefour will make a good base of supply. It was a pleasant surprise to find that the majority of the wines on their shelves cost less than €12, with many priced below €6. I'm sure we'll encounter plenty of pricier bottles while we're in France, but it's nice to be able to treat good wine as a staple rather than an extravagance.

This evening the sun came out and we did some more wandering in the neighborhood. We found a London-based food store called Marks & Spencer with a nice selection of prepared foods that may be useful for eat-in meals. We also stopped in at two venerable local churches: Saint-Sulpice and Saint-Germain-des-Près, both of which will warrant longer visits.

Dinner was at a well-regarded bistro on Rue du Four called Le Pré. It's accustomed to serving American tourists: you can tell because it keeps squirt-bottles of ketchup and yellow mustard on the table. Many French restaurants would cringe at the mere thought of fulfilling a request for these condiments. Even so, the food and the service were good. Peggy had *paillard de poulet* (grilled chicken) and I had grilled *gambas* (prawns) on risotto. It was nice to sit down and have a proper meal served on real plates after a couple days of airline food and catch-as-catch-can snacks. Peggy had a glass of Pouilly Fumé and I had a glass of Côtes de Brouilly Beaujolais that will be worth repeating if we can find it in stores.

The basic plan for today was to arrive in one piece and help our exhausted bodies start to recover from jet lag. Mission accomplished, and then some.

One of the more imposing statues in Luxembourg Garden

FRIDAY, MAY 3

Exploring the Neighborhood

S lept like a rock. Many of the establishments on our little street—especially the bar directly across from us—appear to be student hangouts (we are only a short distance from the Sorbonne) or at least young adult hangouts. But the apartment is well insulated from noise so it's *pas de problème*.

The sun came out mid-morning, just in time for a visit to the Luxembourg Garden, which is a short walk from our apartment. We wandered around a while, bought a sandwich and some *macarons* from a shop called Gérard Mulot, picnicked by the big octagonal pond in front of Luxembourg Palace, then wandered around some more.

Luxembourg Garden is a cross between New York's Central Park and a botanical garden. Each of the huge number of types of trees and flowers is labeled. There are miles of walking paths, lined with statues and flower gardens, which I've read are completely re-planted three times a year, as well as playgrounds, tennis courts, and courts for *boules*. *Boules* (also known as *pétanque*) is basically the French version of bocce ball, played on a groomed dirt/gravel court with fixed dimensions. I've read that it's taken quite seriously in France. There are many tourists in the Garden, but also a lot of Parisians sitting in the sun, reading, eating lunch, jogging, playing chess, and so on. I've had the romantic notion of starting each day with a walk in the Garden followed by a visit to a local *café*. A guy could do worse.

After a brief rain shower we went in search of the shrine of Ina Garten, a/k/a The Barefoot Contessa, a foodie fan favorite whom Peggy adores. Ina and her husband Jeffrey have an apartment on Boulevard Raspail, not far from us. She doesn't publish the address, of course, but she does write about several local shops and markets that help triangulate the general location. We visited one of them, a *boulangerie* called Poilâne, and bought a small loaf of bread for our afternoon wine and cheese. While we were there, a tour group came by—presumably part of a Paris food tour—and the guide explained the shop's connection to Ina. The bread was quite good, by the way.

For dinner, we decided we would simply walk out of the apartment, turn right, stroll around the block, find a place that looked inviting, and eat there. We found no shortage of appealing choices without so much as crossing the street. We settled on a small, intimate bistro called Le Mâchon d'Henri (*Mâchon* as such does not appear in the French dictionary, but *mâchonner* means "chew," so...). We shared an *entrée* (French for what Americans call an appetizer) of goat cheese with pesto and tapenade. For the *plat* (French for what Americans call an entrée or main course), Peggy had salmon with a delicious side composed of fennel and leeks (and cream, to be sure); I had lamb chops that were wonderful. We followed the time-honored practice of simply ordering a *pichet* (pitcher or carafe) of the *vin rouge de la maison* and were not disappointed. They told me what it was and I don't remember. But it was delicious.

We both feel that we are *this close* to being fully adjusted to local time. One more good night's sleep should do it.

Cheese market on Rue du Four.
The cheese monger was straight out of central casting.

SATURDAY, MAY 4

La Marée Verte

I first began to doubt that I had in fact fully adjusted to local time when I woke up at 4:30am. Unable to sleep, I got up and surfed the web until I dozed off again. The second time I woke up was at noon. Obviously yesterday's confidence on this point was premature. I dare to hope that today's extra sleep has done the trick.

We made another run to Carrefour and on the way back stopped at a cheese stand on the street corner. The cheese monger was straight out of central casting. He spoke no English (at least not to us). We would point to something that looked good and he'd cut a small slab for us to taste. When we made our selections he would position a knife over the disk and we'd have to keep indicating smaller and smaller wedges. It was fun. And the cheese was excellent.

As we were walking home a taxi pulled up to the curb in front of a hotel and out climbed our friends Tim and Ruth. They had just completed a river cruise from Amsterdam to Basel, and had tacked on a five-day visit to Paris. We knew they were coming, of course, but being right there to greet them was a happy coincidence.

Later our friends joined us at our apartment. We showed them around and heard all about their cruise, celebrating their arrival with champagne and the cheese we'd just purchased. We then walked them back to their hotel with a brief stop at a *pharmacie*. It felt more like a discount makeup store swarmed by young women; the drug store-type stuff was on the second floor. On the way back Peggy and I browsed a bookstore on Boulevard Saint-Germain. The books were in French, but the look and feel was the same as every other bookstore in the world. A bookstore is always a comfortable place to hang out.

• • •

Dinner was a sentimental journey with a twist. When Peggy and I were here in 2003, one of the first places we ate was a small restaurant at 9 Rue de Pontoise called La Marée Verte. It was a seafood place with a very nice curried mussels appetizer. We liked it so much we went back a second time. Part of the memory was an older woman, presumably the owner, who sat by the door and crooned, as we left, "*Merci à vous! Merci à VOUS!*" We wanted to return there as part of this trip.

And return we did—to 9 Rue de Pontoise. It is no longer La Marée Verte. Online research had disclosed that it had been replaced by another restaurant at the same address called Le Petit Pontoise (the name is an homage to a village on the northern outskirts of Paris). The layout and décor did seem somewhat different. But sixteen years had passed, we reminded ourselves. No doubt the new owner would have remodeled.

I related our story to our hostess (in passable French, if I do say it myself). She had never heard of La Marée Verte but admitted she did not know much about the history of the location. So she called in another staff member. They discussed and debated with one another. The other staff member asked me, "Was there...a woman?" Yes! I said. There was a woman! I remember her! He smiled and said, "That was next door. It is now *un restaurant Italien*."

What happened, as best I can tell, is this. At some point, someone acquired two adjacent properties at 9 Rue de Pontoise. Old photographs that I found online disclose that the new owner converted these properties into two restaurants: Le Petit Pontoise and Le Petit Pontoise Aussi. (*Aussi* means "also." Ann Arbor readers: think "Pizza Bob's" and "Pizza Bob's Uptown.") The "Aussi" location was the former La Marée Verte. At some later time it became an Italian restaurant. We took a peek inside after dinner and the layout did indeed seem more familiar.

We never did get back to the true La Marée Verte. But we got awfully close. And in the end it didn't really matter. Our nostalgia for our previous visit wouldn't have been served by going to an Italian restaurant.

And the whole experience, as it actually unfolded, did the job of bringing back our memories from sixteen years ago.

I should mention that the meal itself was quite good. Quail roasted in a cast iron skillet (*"en cocette"*) for Peggy, grilled veal shank for me. A sturdy house wine, and a delightful wait staff. It made for an indelible memory in its own right.

So to that lovely woman who so warmly welcomed us so long ago, wherever you are: *Merci à vous.*

Detail of Jean d'Aire, one the six men immortalized in Rodin's The Burghers of Calais

SUNDAY, MAY 5

Ina Garten and the Burghers

We met Tim and Ruth at Saint-Sulpice for 9:00am mass. It was at the secondary altar behind the main altar, but even that was imposing. In addition to being a famous cathedral, Saint-Sulpice is also a parish church, and while it was clear that we were not the only tourists in attendance, it was equally clear that the majority of the congregants (I would guess more than 70) were locals. Seven priests concelebrated. It was a diverse group. I later learned that four of them were from Africa, one from Thailand, one from Spain, and one from Ireland. There was a distinct possibility that here, in the capitol of this historically Catholic country that is now one of the most secularized in Europe, we were being ministered to by priests who were, in effect, missionaries, which I found exhilarating. *Le messe* is beautiful in French and I was pleased by the degree to which I was able to follow along with the readings and prayers, and even with the homily.

After mass we had breakfast at Le Pré. Shortly after we were seated a group of eight strapping young Brits walked in, wearing what looked like cycling togs. In fact they were amateur rowers who had just completed a journey all the way from London Tower, down the Thames, across the English Channel, and up the Seine to the Eiffel Tower, in support of a charity. They had literally just gotten out of the water: they were peeling off and changing out of their rowing togs on the spot, and making urgent inquiries about the *toilettes*. They were great fun to talk with.

• • •

We had decided that our main our activity for the day would be a visit to the Musée Rodin, with a stop *en route* to check out the Sunday market in Boulevard Raspail. This put us back in Ina Garten's neighborhood. One of our daughters had told Peggy of a report that Ina and her husband Jeffrey had just returned to Paris from London. As we walked along I suddenly developed the conviction that we were going to see her. We ambled from one end of the market to the other and were just about to leave when I heard a voice somewhere behind me say, "I'm one of your biggest fans..." Peggy heard it too, and turned just in time to see Ina and Jeffrey standing a few feet away. She snapped a photo and off we went. I was thrilled that she had been able to see her hero!

Auguste Rodin is my favorite artist, and his "The Burghers of Calais" my favorite work of art, which inevitably makes the Rodin Museum one of the highest points of any visit to Paris. It was wonderful to tour the house and the gardens again after so many years, and to be able to spend a luxurious amount of time viewing the Burghers from every angle and taking lots of photos. The rest of the group finally dragged me away and we returned home to rest up for the evening.

We ate at Bistro d'Henri, about three doors down from our apartment. Excellent salmon and leeks for Peggy, and beef Bourguignon for me.

• • •

A few interesting restaurant trends have already emerged on this trip. First, it appears that, at least in areas with any significant degree of tourist activity, the traditional slow-paced French dinner has all but disappeared. We've now dined at four different restaurants in the area and all of them served dinner in the manner of a typical American restaurant: we placed our entire order at once and the courses were served one after the other, the main course arriving right on the heels of the entrée. It's not exactly rushed, but it's not the luxurious this-table-is-yours-for-the-evening pace that was *de rigueur* in the past. I suppose we could take the reins and insist on ordering only one course at a time at our own pace. We could also try dining in some less touristy neighborhoods, or look for restaurants that indicate "one seating per evening." Perhaps the concierge at Tim and Ruth's hotel can help us.

Second, there is a distinct sameness to many of the menus. I don't mean only that restaurants offer similar cuisines, or even many of the same dishes, though they do. In one instance the menus themselves—the physical ones—were identical. This happened at Mâchon d'Henri on Friday and then at Bistro d'Henri last night. Of course they are right around the corner from each other, and the back ends of the two houses could well be adjoining. The similarity of the names suggests that they are under common ownership. Even so, you would think Henri might want to differentiate them in some way. The menu at Le Petit Pontoise was not identical in its entirety, but I noticed certain items that were identical—*i.e.*, precisely the same list of *boissons* ("beverages") and the names of particular *aperitifs*.

Third, restaurants in Paris seem to make a point of using the smallest tables possible, no doubt for the sake of squeezing in as many tables as possible. These tables rapidly fill up with plates, bottles, glasses, vases, and the like, creating the need for constant and careful juggling. The end result is not much different from eating from a drop-down tray table on a full-to-capacity airliner—except, of course, that the cuisine is better.

Early rebuilding at Notre-Dame, about three weeks after the devastating fire

MONDAY, MAY 6

Water Lilies, Bistros, and Brasseries

We are racking up an awful lot of steps in Paris. According to Peggy's watch we topped 11,000 yesterday, and scored almost as many today. This is a good thing, as we are also ingesting calories at a prodigious rate.

Today's trek was across the Seine and up through the Tuileries to the Musée de l'Orangerie, so named because it was built on a spot that was once an orange grove. Peggy and I had not been here before. It was built specifically for the purpose of displaying Claude Monet's final masterpiece, *Nymphéas* ("Water Lilies"). Monet actually created more than 250 paintings of water lilies during the last 30 years of his life, all based upon a pond in his garden in Giverny. This particular work consists of eight large murals, depicting water lilies in different settings, in different seasons, and at different times of day. They are mounted on the walls of two adjoining oval galleries with large skylights. Monet gave them to the French government as a symbol of peace on the day after the armistice that concluded World War I. It is fascinating to view them first from a distance and then up close, and to see how the details of brush technique and color selection create the overall impression. The oval presentation places the viewer in the middle of that impression quite effectively.

Downstairs is housed a large private collection of works by numerous impressionists and other painters including Renoir, Cézanne, and Picasso. I bought postcards of two works that grabbed my attention, one by Cézanne and one by Picasso, so that I can learn more about them in the future.

After the museum the four of us had a light lunch at La Dauphine, a small bistro just across the river from the museum, and from there hiked down the Seine to Île Saint-Louis to get a glimpse of Notre-Dame, which is in the very early stages of rebuilding after the terrible fire a few weeks ago. A glimpse is all you can get: all approaches, whether from across the river or on the island itself, are barricaded and heavily guarded.

On the way home Peggy and I stopped in at two Latin Quarter institutions: the venerable Shakespeare and Company, a small, densely-packed, musty marvel of a bookstore, and the Théâtre de la Huchette, which has staged performances of Ionesco's *La Cantatrice Chauve* (The Bald Soprano) and *La Leçon* (The Lesson) every Tuesday through Saturday night, without a single miss, for more than 60 years. Adrian, a friend from my French conversation group who is active in theater, told me about it. We bought tickets to see *Cantatrice* on Friday. I should note that all performances at La Huchette are in French. English subtitles are provided on Wednesdays, but no Wednesday tickets were available. So Peggy is selflessly accommodating me in scratching this particular itch.

• • •

Tonight we dined at Brasserie Vagenende, just a couple blocks away on Boulevard Saint-German. It provided many of the things we found lacking in other restaurants we have visited.

There does not appear to be any generally accepted articulation of the difference between a "bistro" and a "brasserie." Neither designation is official in any sense; establishments are free to adopt either term as they wish. (One writer has said that the only difference between a bistro and a brasserie is that the words are spelled differently.) In very broad terms, a bistro is typically a small, often family-owned and -operated neighborhood establishment with a relatively limited menu, serving only dinner. The four restaurants we've visited so far would comfortably fit this definition of a bistro, whether or not they expressly identified themselves as such.

A brasserie is typically larger, with a more extensive menu, serving lunch as well as dinner with a professional wait staff and on white tablecloths. (A brasserie was originally a brewery—perhaps akin to what is now called a brew pub—though that association has long since disappeared). Brasserie Vagenende matched this description (with somewhat more capacious tables to boot). Interestingly, on an item-per-item basis, prices were not significantly different than at the bistros, though our final bill was higher, partly because we ordered aperitifs and two entrées before our main courses, and partly because all four of us had one of the specials of the day, as well as a bottle of wine rather than a carafe of house wine. Peggy and I both had Dover sole *à la meuniere* (pan-fried); Tim and Ruth both had chateaubriand; all were excellent. And the pace was more relaxed. The concierge at Tim and Ruth's hotel suggested three other restaurants comparable to this one, which we hope to check out.

Inside view of the massive clock in the tower of the Museé d'Orsay

TUESDAY, MAY 7

Orsay and La Dernière Goutte

Today we visited the Musée d'Orsay, probably my favorite museum in the world. It inhabits the former Gare d'Orsay train station, a magnificent structure that has been gloriously adapted to its new use: open, airy, well-lit, and easy to navigate, it is the very antithesis of the dark, stuffy buildings that house many museums around the world. Everything about it feels fresh and unpretentious.

Orsay's artistic charter was to pick up chronologically where the Louvre left off—roughly 1850. This just so happened to position it perfectly to capture the births of Realism, Impressionism, and Neo-Expressionism, and to follow them to the point where they gave rise to Cubism and Modern Art. In short, the Orsay makes a perfect segue from the classics to Picasso and beyond. The only mild downer was that the famous painting of Whistler's Mother (officially titled "Arrangement in Grey and Black No. 1"), which was the creation of an American-born artist with strong ties to France and was committed to the French government from the outset, and which we saw here in 2003, currently resides in the Louvre Abu Dhabi. But no matter. Orsay was five hours very well spent.

Museums come with their own unique breeds of pests: pushy tour guides who monopolize the space in front of major works, and shutterbugs (including obsessive art students) driven by some need to take their very own photo of each and every work in each and every gallery, and to take it from the optimum point of view, even if that point of view happens to be the one that is yours at the moment. I cannot count the number of times one of these clods reached over and stuck an iPhone or iPad directly in front of my face for this purpose.

• • •

The other highlight of the day was a two-hour wine class at a local shop called La Dernière Goutte ("The Last Drop"). Our teacher was Thibault, a youngish former professor of economics at the Sorbonne who has, he says, been a wine geek for more than ten years, a serious oenophile for four years, and owner of the shop—one of the best known in Paris—for two years. The first hour was a lecture, worthy of a French economics professor, about the *terroirs* and business models of the major French wine regions, that soared miles over the heads of all of us. The second hour was the most entertaining wine tasting I've ever participated in. I don't know that I'll ever gain mastery of French wine, but I sure had a fun evening. I think I learned that Languedoc and Gigondas, indeed any wine made from the Grenache grape, will help satisfy my taste for the exotic Châteauneuf-du-Pape but at a more reasonable price.

Dinner was at Fish: La Boissonerie, a fine restaurant around the corner from the wine shop. Peggy and I both had an excellent lamb dish. The wine was a Côtes du Rhône that was very good but that could not help but suffer by comparison to what we'd just experienced with Thibault.

• • •

We've already been here long enough to know that much of what the guidebooks have to say about navigating Paris is wrong, at least for this time of year. We've been able to get into major museums without once standing in long lines, whether for buying tickets, gaining entry, or getting through security. No need for the Paris Museum Pass, and still less for the criminally-overpriced "Paris Pass," which includes the Museum Pass and adds admission to the Eiffel Tower, a ride on a hop-on-hop-off bus tour, and a wall-to-wall Metro pass, for far more than all these things would cost *à la carte*. There may be some justification for the Museum

Pass in July and August, especially for those traveling with children. But I don't see how anyone could slog through enough museums, visit enough monuments, or take enough subway rides in any two- or four- or six-day period, to make a Paris Pass come close to paying for itself.

My thesis will be put to the test tomorrow when we go to Versailles, which is universally described as the ultimate nightmare of crowds, lines, and headaches. Maybe it will be as bad as everyone says. But even if it is, it will impact only one day of a trip that until now has been blessedly relaxed.

The Hall of Mirrors

WEDNESDAY, MAY 8

Versailles

To be candid, I have never had much interest in Versailles and I have to admit that after being there today my level of interest did not increase one iota. But like the Louvre and the Eiffel Tower it is worth doing once, if only to be able to say you did it and to know you will never need to do it again.

All the guidebooks say that getting to Versailles is a breeze—you just hop onto the RER (high-speed commuter train) and 37 minutes later, *voila*: you're there. Except, it turns out, on May 8, which is a French national holiday. Versailles itself is open for business on May 8. The RER on the other hand is not, as we learned the hard way. We set out for the local RER station at 8:00am, having tickets for a 9:00am entry to Versailles. Two hours, four stations, and two Metro lines later, we straggled into the Versailles courtyard, dazed and frazzled before we'd even got inside.

Versailles is one of the world's most spectacular monuments to decadence and wretched excess. That's not exactly an insult: it was *designed* that way. Louis XIV believed that the sheer magnitude and splendor of the palace and grounds would persuade visiting foreign dignitaries that France was a power to be reckoned with.

We spent the morning filing through room after room after room filled with massive but undistinguished paintings and bedecked in endless gold-leaf filigree, cosseted by the usual horde of polyglot tour groups and industrious shutterbugs. To my knowledge there is not a single famous or noteworthy work of art in the whole place, though the Hall of Mirrors and the massive gardens are striking.

After a quick lunch in the Angelina café—featuring its signature rich dark cocoa—we slogged around those gardens during a brief, merciful interlude in an otherwise steady rain. Then, having solemnly assured ourselves that we had done our duty, we got back on the train for home.

• • •

After a much-needed nap we met up with Tim and Ruth for dinner at The Frog and Princess, a British micro-brew pub across the street from our apartment. (There are also two Irish pubs on the block.) The beers, burgers, and fish & chips (that's me!) were first rate and a nice change from Paris bistro and brasserie fare.

We then bid farewell to our good friends, who after a thirteen-day cruise down the Rhine and five days in Paris were battling head colds and ready to head home in the morning. It was wonderful to be able to share several days with them in this glorious city.

THE MAN WITH THE BAGUETTE

Le Bon Marché, the world's first modern-style department store

THURSDAY, MAY 9

The Umbrellas of Paris

Rest day. We spent a drizzly morning at home sipping coffee and reading—in my case, plowing through Ionesco's *La Cantatrice Chauve* (in French) in preparation for attending tomorrow night's performance. We went wandering for a while this afternoon, our only destinations being the grand Paris department store Le Bon Marché and its affiliated foodie-fantasy emporium, La Grande Épicerie. It was a near case of sensory overload. Honestly: if vegetables had been that gorgeous when we were growing up, I'd have eaten more of them. We also reconnoitered a couple establishments on our list of wanna-do restaurants. They looked great, of course, and no doubt *are* great. If only we had six months in Paris instead of two weeks.

This evening we enjoyed a salad and a nice Sancerre at Mabillon, on Boulevard Saint-Germain, belatedly getting our first outdoor café experience. Not the last! Afterwards we took a pleasant stroll through the Rue de Buci and Rue de Seine neighborhoods, spying many interesting restaurants and art galleries that deserve further exploration. Beautiful, cool, calm evening, perfect for both activities.

Rue du Four at night

FRIDAY, MAY 10

Picasso and The Bald Soprano

At last a sunny morning! We had planned to get up and out early, and thank heaven we did because the "public works" project arrived with a roar at 9:00am sharp in the form of an enormous jackhammer attacking the pavement directly below our window. It lasted only 20 minutes or so but would have made for a novel wake-up call.

We had coffee and croissants at Paul, a lovely café on Rue du Four. We had the good fortune of meeting a charming couple from Nashville who were sitting next to us. We'd overheard them discussing Vaucluse, the part of Provence we will be visiting. They have been there before, including a visit to Isle-sur-la-Sorgue, the town we will be staying in. Indeed, they are headed there tomorrow and will be in Isle-sur-la-Sorgue for its big open-air market on Sunday. Ophelia had very nice French. George, as it happens, is a retired federal bankruptcy judge who knows several of my former Nashville law colleagues. All in all, it was one of those delightful encounters that sometimes come your way.

• • •

The main event for the day was a long stroll down the Boulevard Saint-Germain, across Île Saint-Louis, and into the Marais district. *Marais* means "swamp," indicative of what used to be there. It is now one of the trendiest and most cosmopolitan parts of the city. A full day was barely enough to scratch the surface. We started at the Place des Vosges, a lovely park surrounded by elegant luxury apartment buildings most of whose ground floors house oh-so-trendy art galleries, and then made our way to the Picasso Museum.

The thing about any Picasso exhibition is that there were at least a dozen different Picassos, depending on the time period, with many different styles and subject matters, and hundreds of examples of each. You're never sure which Picasso(s) you will encounter in any particular collection. Some of them I like, others I try to understand and appreciate, and still others leave me cold.

At the moment more than half the Picasso Museum space is devoted to an exhibit contemplating the similarities between Picasso and Alexander Calder, the American artist known primarily for his mobiles. I rather enjoy Calder's work, which is a good thing because about 70 percent of the pieces in the "joint" exhibit are his, and about 90 percent of the material in the audio guide was about him.

As for the rest of the museum, the bulk of the works were low-profile scatterlings from various periods in Picasso's career that don't do much for me. We later learned that the museum's Picasso collection consists primarily of pieces that were squirreled away in attics and basements when he died, and sold by the family to pay off his debts.

We enjoyed walking the Marais. I suspect there's much more to be seen there, and we may well wander over there again before we leave.

• • •

A few bits of serendipity from today's hike:

- We walked by the Hotel Agora, where we stayed during our first visit to Paris sixteen years ago. It was nice to see the old neighborhood again, including the square where we encountered The Man with the Baguette, who inspired this trip.

- We happened by the showroom of Laguiole, a famous maker of high-end cutlery. High-priced, too: there was an ivory-handled wine bottle opener in the window priced at €445. I don't buy wine nearly good enough to justify the use of such a tool.

• We got ice cream cones at Berthillon: white chocolate for me and salted caramel cream for Peggy. My brother-in-law Mike swears that Berthillon makes the best ice cream on the planet and I think he may be right.

Tonight was our night to contribute to the ongoing legend of La Théâtre de la Huchette. It is small, dark, crowded, and located on one of the cheesiest streets in the Latin Quarter. The time spent reading *La Cantatrice Chauve* paid off in that I had a general idea of what was going on, even though I could not hope to follow all the dialogue. This was no small handicap given that the play is essentially one long series of word plays (in French!), but the direction and acting were so strong that it was easy to enjoy the production anyway.

For dinner we checked out La Grande Crèmerie, a small-plate restaurant with farm-to-table food, natural wines, and rustic atmosphere. We shared an Iberian meat board with selected cheeses and breads. Highly recommended.

*Wines from La Dernière Goutte,
one of the best-known wine shops in Paris*

SATURDAY, MAY 11

Anniversaire de Mariage

Today is our 45th wedding anniversary. Could there possibly be a better place to celebrate it than Paris? Fittingly enough, the weather has been rainy/sunny/rainy/sunny all day—just like our wedding day.

We stayed inside this morning and relaxed until the sun came out about 11:00, then took a long, aimless walk around Saint-Germain. We turned into whatever streets looked interesting, checked out a few stores, and hid under a couple awnings when the rain occasionally returned. Much of our itinerary led us around and through Luxembourg Garden. We discovered a small anglophone bookstore on Rue de Médicis called The Red Wheelbarrow, and enjoyed chatting with the owner, Penelope, who is originally from Canada but has operated a bookstore in Paris for many years. We then had a cup of French onion soup and a glass of wine at Au Petite Suisse, providing outdoor seating with nice views of the Garden just across Rue de Vaugirard, and of the Théâtre l'Odéon next door.

Then back to La Dernière Goutte, which was hosting a wine tasting featuring two small "natural" (organic) vintners. The first, Lacroix-Vanel, is located in Pézanas, a small town not far from Montpelier in the south. We chatted with the winemaker, Marc-Olivier Bertrand, and chose a 2015 Languedoc they call Mélanie. The second vintner, Chateau Moulin Pey-Labrie, is located in Fronsac, in the Bordeaux region. We talked with Bénédicte Hubau who, with her husband Grégoire, produces the wines, and chose a 2010 Merlot blend. Neither of these wines is currently available in the U.S.; I suppose the vintners are too small to have attracted a U.S. importer yet.

We asked Thibault, the proprietor, to recommend a Châteauneuf-du-Pape, and he steered us to a bottle from Clos de Mont-Olivet, a label that *is* available in the U.S. By virtue of its 2011 vintage, Thibault said, it was ready to drink now. We brought this bottle home from France and will open it as a way of recalling our time in Paris.

Thibault also taught us a very useful lesson about "bad" wine. We mentioned that we had on occasion dumped a bottle of wine—usually one that had sat in our cellar beyond the ideal "drink-by" date—that didn't taste right when we opened it. Slightly aghast, he told us that the next time that happened, we should simply set the open bottle aside and let the wine "work" for 24 or even 48 hours. I'm happy to report that we've had good success with this method.

• • •

We had dinner at L'Îlot Vache, one of our favorite restaurants from 16 years ago. We used Uber to get there—it works just as well in Paris as it does in the States.

The meal was fantastic. For starters, a wonderful terrine-plus-salad entrée. For Peggy, chateaubriand with three sauces; for me, rack of lamb with Provençal spices; an excellent red wine; and a relaxed pace that allowed ample time to savor all of it. A bonus was sharing the evening with a couple from Connecticut at the table next to us. They were making a one-day stop in Paris on the way back from a cruise of the Greek islands. Another bonus: we had mentioned to the hostess that we were celebrating our anniversary, and the restaurant marked the occasion by presenting our dessert—a chocolate lava cake with Berthillon ice cream—topped with a large volcano-like sparkler.

We have now been in Paris just over a week. Most of the items on our (deliberately minimal) wanna-do lists have been covered. We can sense that the deep purpose of the trip is being fulfilled: a decisive break with the routines and responsibilities of the past; a new sense of what sort of lifestyle could "work" for us; a rediscovery of who we are, individually and together, and of who we can be. Much remains to be discovered: we have another full week here, and Provence still awaits.

*Saint-Germain-des-Prés, our neighborhood church
and the oldest church in Paris*

SUNDAY, MAY 12

Saint-Germain-des-Près and the Marais

Today was the first day since we arrived without so much as a hint of rain. It was cool but sunny almost all day and we tried to make the most of it.

This morning we went to mass at Saint-Germain-des-Près, just a few blocks from the apartment. It is, we learned, the oldest church in Paris. The side aisles are undergoing substantial renovation but the nave, the transept, and the choir area behind the main altar are all open. The natural light is glorious and the rose windows are spectacular.

Notwithstanding its guidebook status, Saint-Germain-des-Près is a genuine parish church. I would estimate that more than 250 people were present. I'm sure we weren't the only visitors, but for the most part it looked like any other congregation you might see in any other Catholic church on any other Sunday morning: lots of families, teenagers, young adults, and crying babies. There was one celebrant, along with a deacon, and eleven(!) altar boys. The cantor, the readers, and the eucharistic ministers all looked like regular moms and dads, many of them in blue jeans. Today was special in that there were two baptisms. The *baptisées* were not infants but young boys who looked to be about 10 years old. I don't whether this is the norm in France or not. All in all it was a very comfortable experience—if we lived around here, we would be glad to make this our parish.

After mass we went to La Crêpe Ris du Clown, one of several *crêperies* on the nearby Rue des Cannettes. I know enough French to "get" the joke embedded in the name: *ris* means smile, and there is a figure of a laughing clown in the entryway. Thus we are in the Crêperie of the Laughing Clown. We sat outside and enjoyed *galettes* with eggs, cheese, ham, and several wonderful spices. When they arrived we thought we might have over-ordered, but they were light and delicate and when we left we felt satisfied but not stuffed.

• • •

This afternoon we decided to check out one of the tours offered by an agency called Walk Paris, which was recommended by the owner of The Red Wheelbarrow and is well-reviewed by numerous guidebooks. Today's choice was a walking tour of the northern part of the Marais district. It was an excellent tour covering a number of interesting places, none of which we could possibly have noticed or appreciated on our own. Our guide was Chloe, a London native who has lived in Paris since she was 18. Walk Paris offers a number of intriguing tours; I suspect we will patronize them again this week.

I should note that we got to and from the Marais using the Paris bus system. It is an extremely comprehensive, well-organized, and reasonably priced way of getting around. It uses the same ticket as the Metro and the RER but stops are far more numerous and conveniently located (the stop for the 96 line is less than 100 yards from our front door), and it can get you where you're going a lot faster than the Metro if—as was the case today—your start and end points are on the same bus line, thus avoiding a transfer. Of course the bus is affected by traffic conditions more than the Metro, as we learned today. Our ride to the Marais took less than 15 minutes. But Sunday is a very busy day in central Paris, and the vehicular and (especially) pedestrian traffic in the late afternoon was horrible. The return trip took 45 minutes and the bus was jammed, bringing back dark memories of the time I caught a guy trying to pick my pocket on a crowded bus in Rome on a Sunday. No such incident today—or any other day, for that matter. There is very little street crime in Paris, but the city does have a reputation for being rife with pickpockets. We've tried to walk a line between carelessness on the one hand and paranoia on the other.

After ten days of restaurant dining, we finally got around to something we had wanted to incorporate into our "live a month in France" motif: we made a trip to the grocery store and then made dinner at the apartment. Very tasty, very relaxing. We mostly bought prepared foods from Marks & Spencer, but also picked up a fresh-baked baguette from the *boulangerie* across the street. Thus did I, at long last, become "the man with the baguette."

Paris Apartment

We've been living in this apartment for ten days now. The verdict is in: we love it. It is compact but comfortable. It appears to have been completely remodeled very recently. The contemporary styling makes full use of venerable stone pillars and wooden beams. The kitchen and bathrooms are fully up to date with the latest plumbing and appliances. The second bedroom/bathroom is wonderful: it provides extra closet space and allows us to use separate bathrooms and dressing rooms—an unexpected luxury that would be awfully easy to get used to. The beds are comfortable. The apartment is remarkably soundproof; we get some street noise in the main living area, but none in the bedroom.

The main living area is fully furnished, unlike many properties we explored, which upon careful examination appeared to have no couches or sitting chairs. Interestingly, the couches, side chairs, and beds are several inches lower than we're used to. Not just in our apartment: we've consistently noticed the same thing in furniture stores. Dining tables and chairs are pretty much the same as back home.

The owners and the management were thoughtful enough to provide a grocery cart, two umbrellas, several AC adaptors, and even a portable wi-fi device (the French call it *wee-fee*). The upstairs neighbor plays the piano but only in the afternoons, and well enough that it is a pleasure to listen to. We pick up some quiet rumbling from the Metro, but this is not a major issue.

The location is likewise excellent. The Sixth Arrondissement, especially south of the Boulevard Saint-Germain, has a good mix of tourist and non-tourist atmosphere. We have the glorious Luxembourg Garden virtually in our back yard, and are close to Saint-Sulpice and

Saint-Germain-des-Près. We can easily walk to everything from the Musée Rodin and the Boulevard Raspail market to the west, to the Musée D'Orsay, Tuileries, Louvre, and Musée de L'Orangerie to the north, as well as to the Latin Quarter (and, if we are feeling spry, the Îles and even the Marais) to the east. Metro and bus lines are close by. There are two grocery stores and several specialty markets in close proximity. Rue Princesse is part of a cluster of small streets comprising a lively district of cafés, bars, and bistros. When (not if!) we return, our interests will likely be even less touristic than now, and we might look either toward the 7th Arrondissement, where the Rodin Museum is located, to the neighborhood south of the Luxembourg Garden, or to the area around the Odéon theatre. (Our visits to the Marais have confirmed the hunch that it's more crowded and frenetic than we're looking for.) But all in all we have a great many likes, and very few dislikes, about this spot.

One of the greenhouses on Île de la Cité

MONDAY, MAY 13

Flâneurs

French culture celebrates a character called the *flâneur*. Technically the word means "loafer," but more generally it connotes an "aimless wanderer." There are books and articles that suggest that the best way to explore Paris is to simply strike out with no fixed itinerary in mind, go wherever curiosity leads, turn down a side street when you spy something interesting, stop in at places that catch your imagination, and spend as much or as little time as you like at each stop along the way. In short: wander aimlessly.

Today Peggy and I became *flâneurs*. It was a beautiful morning with no rain in the forecast. We had not yet toured the 1st Arrondissement, on the Right Bank of the Seine, so we took off in that general direction, the only particular destination being a kitchen supply store favored by Ina Garten. By the end of the day we had:

- Crossed the Pont des Arts with beautiful views up and down the Seine, its lampposts encircled with clusters of small padlocks bearing the names or initials of couples bearing witness to their love.

- Strolled through the massive courtyard behind the Louvre, surrounded by the Colonnade de Perrault.

- Made our way to E. Dehillerin, the aforementioned kitchen supply store. It is basically a small, old, cramped warehouse that caters mainly to professional chefs, though there were plenty of regular-looking folks like us poking around.

- Drifted through Les Halles, passing by Église Saint-Eustache and dropping into some shops in the Forum Les Halles.

- Meandered down Rue Les Halles to Rue Rivoli and the Place du Châtelet, where we sat for a while in a small wooded park we'd never heard of, the Square de la Tour Saint-Jacques. The tower, the only remnant of a medieval church, is striking. An island of serenity in one of Paris's busiest areas.

- Crossed the Pont de Change, with a nice view of the Eiffel Tower in the distance, and one of l'Hôtel de Ville (City Hall) just across the river, onto Île de la Cité, where we:

- Happened upon a remarkable event called *La Fête du Pain*, sponsored by a group called Les Boulangers de Paris. It featured two enormous tents, each housing large groups of professional bakers preparing an enormous variety of breads, pastries, and even pizzas. The fruits of their labors were sold on the spot at extremely reasonable prices, with the proceeds going to support the hungry. One of the most interesting activities was

- A competition to determine The Best Baguette in France. (Now that's something to ponder!) Bakers from all over the country competed. We watched as they labored away, kneading and rolling the dough, oh-so-carefully shaping, weighing, and measuring the loaves, intently monitoring the ovens, all under the watchful eyes of professional judges. Next door to all this activity were:

- Several rows of block-long walk-through greenhouses with stunning arrays of fresh-cut flowers, plants, and related items. Going back and forth from the aroma of the bread to the scent of the flowers was a sensory delight. In due course we

- Made our way across the street to the Brasserie Les Deux Palais for lunch, featuring two Paris standbys: for Peggy a quiche Lorraine; for me a *Crocque Monsieur* ("Crunch for the Gentleman"), a grilled ham-and-cheese sandwich with the cheese on top rather than in the middle. There is, of course, a counterpart for the lady: a *Crocque Madame*, basically the same sandwich but with an egg included.

- Ventured down several streets near Notre-Dame, getting as close a look at the Cathedral as the *gendarmes* would allow.

- Crossed the Pont Saint-Louis onto Île Saint-Louis, and walked down Rue Saint-Louis en l'Île (one does detect a theme in the nomenclature) which bisects the island. It would take a tour guide to do it justice as most of the points of interest are historic in a way not perceivable to the visiting eye.

- Crossed the Pont de la Tournelle to the Latin Quarter.

- Perused the *bouquinistes* (technically "booksellers," though the distinctive green metal stalls sell many other wares as well) along the Left Bank until we

- Reached Shakespeare and Company. Peggy looked for a couple books she had heard of. I went upstairs to confirm for my brother-in-law Phil that the beat-up old piano he saw there years ago is indeed still there.

- Paid a leisurely visit to the beautiful Église Saint-Séverin and then, almost six hours after we set out,

- Wended our way past the Théâtre de l'Odéon and back to our apartment, with a brief stop at Marks & Spencer to replenish our wine supply.

I wholeheartedly agree that playing the *flâneur* is the best way to explore Paris. Except for Ina's favorite cookware store, we had none of these places or experiences in mind when we began the day; indeed we had never even heard of many of them. I can't wait to do more aimless wandering.

• • •

Dinner tonight at La Boussole ("The Compass"), a neighborhood bistro with a Thai spin. The entrée was a seafood casserole with what tasted like a curry cream sauce. It was one of the best dishes we've had, if they served it as a main course we'd go back for it in a heartbeat. Main courses were good: chicken for Peg, marinated beef for me, and a good house red.

Inside the Abbey Bookshop

TUESDAY, MAY 14

Rue Cler and Beyond

We set out this morning by bus for Rue Cler. Some descriptions make it sound like a major outdoor market. In fact it is a nice pedestrian thoroughfare lined with shops, food stores, and cafés. It was quiet when we arrived, so we *flâneured* off and eventually found our way to

- Champs de Mars, the park that is essentially the front yard of

- The Eiffel Tower. Lines didn't look too bad but we did it the last time and didn't feel the need to repeat. On to

- The Place du Trocadéro, which many say has the best views of the Eiffel Tower. We turned right and moved on to

- L'Arc de Triomphe. It sits in the middle of a massive traffic circle and can be reached only via a subterranean pedestrian walkway from which, for €12, you are allowed to ascend into daylight and, well, walk around under the Arch. Pass. We proceeded to

- The Champs Élysées, which is both Rodeo Drive on *stéroïdes* and also home to an assortment of more pedestrian establishments. When we passed a McDonalds we decided to hop on the bus from hell (traffic was horrible) back to

- Rue Cler, where we had a *salade* at the Cookie-Cutter Café (not its real name but we are beginning to notice a certain sameness), after which we bought some astonishingly delicious *fraises* and *pêches*, and several delightful *fromages* as well.

We cooled our heels at the apartment for a bit and then sallied forth into Saint-Germain in search of some vintage maps of Paris (actually, reproductions thereof). First stop was San Francisco Book Company, a small, claustrophobic bookstore not far from our apartment. No luck. Second stop was The Abbey Bookshop, an even more claustrophobic store closer to the Latin Quarter, where the owner let us buy a single page from a book about the history of Paris. It's not exactly what I had in mind but it will do for now.

We discovered an indoor mall of specialty shops in back of the Marks & Spencer shop. How we have managed to be here for more than ten days without noticing this is hard to imagine. We were able to add some sliced *viandes* and a delicious terrine to our previous purchases, as well as a fresh baguette. It all made for a sumptuous feast at our apartment.

Saint-Denys, the first bishop of Paris. Legend has it that after he was martyred he carried his head to the spot where his statue now stands.

WEDNESDAY, MAY 15

Montmartre

We went to Montmartre when we were here sixteen years ago but the visit was brief and unsatisfying. Basically we took a bus that rolled north through the X-rated area around the Moulin Rouge, rode the funicular up to Sacré Cœur, saw the tacky trinket sellers and cheesy artists camped out around the basilica, got turned off, and went back home.

This time we took a guided walking tour and the results were immeasurably better. We again used Walk Paris and again drew Chloe as our guide. She has lived in Montmartre for years and is well versed in the lore of the area. We started at the Abbesses Metro stop, and from there made our way, at a very gentle pace, to the top of the butte. Highlights included:

- The Metro stop itself, which is one of the better examples of the *art nouveau* design that many Metro stops share.

- The "I Love You" wall, featuring that expression painted in 311 languages.

- The brick church of St. John the Evangelist (noteworthy because brick construction is not common in Paris).

- Le Bateau Lavoir (the "laundry boat"), where Picasso and many of his contemporaries lived in their starving-artist days.

- Exemplars of the "Wallace Fountains" that are found throughout the city.

- The Moulin Galette, the first of the then-30 windmills atop the butte to realize that serving food and (especially) drink could be a moneymaker.

- The statue of the *Passe-Muraille,* a literary character who could walk through walls.

- The statue of Saint-Denys, the first bishop of Paris. He was martyred by beheading, and legend has it that he immediately picked up his head and walked six miles to the spot where the statue—which shows him carrying his head in his hands—now stands.

- The famous Lapin Agile café, once frequented by Picasso among other artists.

- And of course the Sacré-Cœur Basilica, which occupies the highest point in the city.

Chloe led us through all this while carefully sidestepping the trinket shops and artist galleries, which are world-famous pickpocket cherry patches.

After the tour we had lunch at the Restaurant Au Soleil de Montmartre, one of a number of places near Sacré-Cœur that Chloe said were more oriented to locals than to tourists, and then visited the Musée de Montmartre, which holds a number of recognized Montmartre pieces, such as the Chat Noir posters and the painting of the Lapin Agile.

After a breather at the apartment we revisited our friend Penelope at The Red Wheelbarrow, where Peggy had ordered a book about Degas's fourteen-year-old dancer, then dropped into one of the many Gibert book emporiums to pick up a road map of Provence (I wasn't entirely sure how well GPS would work there) and the book featuring the story of the *Le passe-muraille,* which Chloe said was a useful read for learning French.

We ended the day too pooped to even try to settle on a dinner spot and so repaired to the apartment for a reprise of last night's meat/cheese/terrine/bread feast. Oh so good!

Bouquinistes *along the Left Bank*

THURSDAY, MAY 16

The Seine, the Panthéon, and Le Christine

This morning we took a cruise on the Seine. We debated it—frankly, most of the tours looked a bit cheesy—but decided what the heck. The Vedette cruise line was recommended and while I have nothing to compare it to, ours was fine. A boat provides a different vantage point of familiar sights, even if it's not a particularly *good* vantage point. But it was yet another spectacular day and for €20 it was a pleasant ride.

One particularly good aspect was that the boat cruised further east past Île Saint-Louis than we had previously walked, which enabled us to discover the Jardin Tino-Rossi, which runs for a half-mile or so along the Left Bank and features lots of walking paths and gardens. It is also home to the Musée de Sculpture en Plein Air, which includes a number of modern pieces in outdoor settings, which is how all sculpture should be displayed. We headed there after the cruise, stopping *en route* at the Fête de Pain we'd visited before. We redeemed our previous oversight by buying a *sandwich de poulet* on a fresh baguette and a *tarte aux cerises,* and then picnicked along the Seine amid glorious flowers, trees, and sculptures.

On the way home we made a more extensive tour of the bouqinistes along the Left Bank across from the two islands. I was still hoping to find a reproduction of a vintage map of Paris, and maybe one of the part of Provence we will be visiting. I did find a map of the Vaucluse district but it didn't include Isle-sur-la-Sorgue. I may try again tomorrow. It's got to be out there somewhere.

We concluded today's tour with a visit to the Panthéon, a truly impressive structure in which are interred many of France's greatest heroes, whether military, political, religious, scientific, or cultural. Only a country whose history is measured in centuries can have such a monument. The Panthéon also devotes considerable space to veneration of Sainte Genevieve, the patron saint of Paris, with whom we had not been acquainted prior to this visit, although she makes frequent appearances in local culture including a striking statue on the Pont Tournelle. Other worthies interred in the Pantheon include Jean-Jacques Rousseau, Victor Hugo, Emile Zola, and the Curies.

Despite our best efforts to block it out, the thought has inevitably intruded on us that tomorrow will be our last full day in Paris, and that at least some of it must be spent preparing to leave. The plan is to forego any more museums, monuments, and tours, and simply enjoy being here, perhaps revisiting a few favorite local spots. *C'est bien triste.*

• • •

We had a truly wonderful dinner at Le Christine, which had been recommended by the concierge at Tim and Ruth's hotel. They offered a couple *menus*, which in France refers to a prix-fixe meal, usually with your choice of which entrée, which main course, and which dessert. There was another option with the tantalizing name <<Trust the Chef>>. We couldn't pass that up. Tonight the chef served:

- An *amuse-bouche* featuring trout and trout roe.

- An entrée of oysters, mushrooms, and grilled duck breast, served with a terrific white wine called *Cascade*.

- First course of salmon with sweet potato purée and a rich crème sauce.

- Second course of veal chop served with a very nice red Sancerre.

- Dessert of roasted pear drizzled with salted butter caramel and served with vanilla ice cream (anything but "plain").

We've had some very good meals in some very nice restaurants over the past two weeks, but our next trip to Paris will definitely include a return visit to Le Christine.

Pétanque *match in Luxembourg Garden*

FRIDAY, MAY 17

Au Revoir à Paris

We decided to forego any major excursions today in favor of simply enjoying the neighborhood and doing things we'd wanted to do, or to do again, but hadn't yet gotten around to.

I started the day with mass at Saint-Sulpice. (Attending daily mass in Paris had been one of my romantic notions for this trip. At least I managed to get there once.) There were about 50 people there. Afterwards I spent some time looking at the various side chapels and the art and statuary. One chapel was dedicated to St. Charles Borromeo—the only time I can remember encountering the namesake of my boyhood parish in St. Charles, Missouri. There was also a bulletin board with pictures of the pastoral staff, which included priests from Cameroons, Togo, the Congo, and several other exotic places including New Delhi.

While we're on the subject: another of my failed romantic notions was taking a daily early-morning walk in the Luxembourg Garden, followed by a *café crème* at some local café that I had adopted as my own. Most days we were too pooped for any early-morning activity. The one time I did go out before 8:00am I was surprised to discover that almost no Paris cafés open until 10:00 or 11:00 or even noon. Perhaps there will be more opportunity to fulfill this dream in Provence.

Galettes for brunch at La Crêperie des Canettes. Mailed postcards to the kids so they'd have a Paris postmark. Walked down the Boulevard, back along the Seine, made another fruitless search of the bouquinistes for some maps or sketches or something. I'm ticked off at myself that I didn't start on this sooner. Took a couple pictures we'd forgotten to take earlier. Check, check, check. Laundry, organizing, and packing for tomorrow's journey to Provence: check.

• • •

We took a farewell stroll through the Luxembourg Garden this evening. It was filled with little kids playing on the swings and sailing boats in the pond, old men reading books and playing chess, and men and women of all descriptions having serious *pétanque* matches. It's a simple game but it does require skill. And these guys (including a handsome gentleman in a stylish Parisian suit) were very, *very* good at it.

On the way home we passed Saint-Sulpice and I remembered that it was hosting a performance of Dvorak's oratorio *Stabat Mater* this evening. We had made dinner reservations at Le Procope, which is the oldest café in Paris (though it's not really just a café any more) but were having a hard time working up any enthusiasm for it. Frankly, last night's dinner at Le Christine was an awfully hard act to follow. We decided to call an audible on fourth down and go to the show.

The performance was glorious, moving, and, well, *long*. Oratorios like *Stabat Mater* or Handel's *Messiah* are an acquired taste, one that I freely admit I haven't acquired and probably never will. But to be to able to witness 150-plus incredibly talented artists collaborating on something so massive and complex, in such a splendid and inspiring setting, is a very rare treat. Quite a send-off from Paris!

The stairs to the apartment

Final Reflections on Paris

After a somewhat chilly/rainy first week, the weather since last Sunday has consistently been nothing short of spectacular: sunny, mostly cloudless, deep blue skies, and temperatures in the 60s (F) every day.

- The "public works" project has continued throughout our stay. Having a jackhammer roar to life directly below your window at 9:00am certainly gets your attention, though it's only happened a couple times and never lasts more than 20 minutes or so. I've come to think of it as just another aspect of what "living in Paris" would be like.

- As I write this, the classical pianist who lives upstairs is in the midst of one of her occasional practice sessions. It is delightful. We have enjoyed it throughout our stay.

- I put a lot of time and effort, for more than six months before our trip, into retrieving the French I'd learned in high school and college, plus learning a whole lot more. I don't regret a minute of it; it was fun, an interesting intellectual challenge, and I've met some delightful people in the process. But the fact is that there hasn't been much opportunity to use it in Paris. I can be identified as an American from a *kilomètre* away, and with very few exceptions every Parisian I have encountered has spoken English pretty (or very) well. I'd feel I was imposing if I asked them to humor my poor skills. I also suspect that many of them are happy for an opportunity to practice their English. Perhaps my newly gained language skills will be of more use in Provence. *On verra.*

• Peggy and I have both commented that we've gotten a little worn down by the noise and crowds and traffic of Paris, which of course was due in large part to our own choice to stay in a busy area and to venture out into the city most days. Next time we could stay in a quieter area and do less adventuring, and we crossed so many items off our wanna-do list on this trip that a more laid-back approach might actually be possible. In any event, we are looking forward to what we trust will be the slower pace of life in Provence.

Isle-sur-la-Sorgue's signature water wheel, one of more than a dozen encircling the old town

SATURDAY, MAY 18

On to Provence

Up early. Uber to Gare de Lyon, high-speed TGV train to Avignon, rental car to Isle-sur-la-Sorgue. Everything went smoothly but there were enough moving parts to manage, and enough potential mishaps to avoid, that I was a bit frazzled by the time we arrived.

Isle-sur-la-Sorgue (generally referred to simply as "Isle" by the natives) is in the Vaucluse district of Provence, more specifically in the area known as the Luberon because of its proximity to the Luberon Mountains to the north. The town is, as its name suggests, an island in the Sorgue River, a swift-running, crystal-clear stream whose source is in the hills about eight kilometers to the east. It splits into two streams that come back together about two kilometers to the west, creating the small island on which the town was originally established. Several small rivulets criss-cross the island. Isle's history as a mill town is evidenced by a number of vintage water wheels scattered around the island.

Our apartment is located on the Rue des Bernardins, on the *premier étage* above a gift shop, with a small balcony overlooking the street. We were greeted by the owner of the apartment, Eva, and took our time getting unpacked and settling in.

When we arrived this afternoon, Isle was rockin'. Shops, cafés, and restos were humming. Streets were filled with pedestrians and the occasional car. Even when you crossed the river into the surrounding town, traffic was difficult. Then, suddenly, at about 7:00pm everything went dead. All the shops closed, as did most of the restaurants, and the streets were nearly deserted. On Saturday night! I would ordinarily expect a town to be more, not less, active on a Saturday night, especially when the biggest event of the week—The Market—is the next day. But maybe that's not the Provençal way.

This may well be the calm before the storm. Isle-sur-la-Sorgue is renowned for its Sunday market, which is one of the largest in the region. Eva's words of orientation included a stern admonition to get our vehicle off the island Saturday evening lest it be towed away during the night, and her gentle but clear recommendation was to forego any plans that involved using the car until Monday, as getting in and out of town by car on Sunday would be a headache. So we have been duly warned and, having removed the car to an outlying parking lot, we are prepared to stand sideways and brace ourselves for whatever onslaught may face us tomorrow morning.

• • •

Of the few restaurants that were open this evening, we opted for Brasserie Le Bellevue, which is one of many on the Quai Jean Jauré (one of the main drags on the island) with a view of, and tables on the bank of, the river. Both of us were exhausted and we picked the Bellevue precisely because it was nothing special—reviewers tended to describe it with words like "reasonable" and "reliable"—and mostly empty at 8:00pm. What we got was one of the better meals of the trip so far. I had trout and Peggy had salmon and they were both prepared to perfection, grilled crispy on the outside, amazingly tender and juicy on the inside, with subtle hints of butter and Provençal spices. If this cuisine is indeed "nothing special," I can't wait to see what lies ahead.

Sunday market in Isle-sur-la-Sorgue (Notre-Dame-des-Anges in the background)

SUNDAY, MAY 19

Market Day

We went to mass this morning at the local Catholic church, Notre-Dame-des-Anges. It is surprisingly large and splendid for such a small town. As in the other churches we've visited, communion is handled differently than in the U.S. People do not come forward row-by-row, but in a seemingly random fashion. Wine is not used. Most people take the host in their hands but a few either genuflect or kneel and receive it on the tongue. The two Paris churches we visited had rather odd kneelers that looked like miniature cane chairs facing backwards. This church had no kneelers of any kind. Most people stand during the parts of the mass when kneeling is conventional, but a few kneel on the floor.

After mass we walked through the Sunday market. It is indeed a significant undertaking. The island, where we are staying, is a labyrinth of streets that range from small, to very small, to tiny. All of the larger streets, all of the squares, and some of the smaller streets, were lined with stands. Most of the goods are the usual: produce, cheese, meats, breads, clothing, artisan goods, linens. But there were a few unusual stands: one with an astonishing array of drawer pulls, another for power gardening tools. We bought a roasted chicken, some asparagus, two cheeses, a baguette, and some strawberries. When we got home Peggy put together a very nice repast. Sunday dinner, Provence style!

Afterwards we relaxed at the apartment and later took a walk around the island to get our bearings. Along the way we saw the numerous old water wheels that are the village's historical calling card; discovered a medium-sized "U Utile" supermarket within easy walking distance (from which I carried baguettes home several times); and walked by the antiques district, a warren of stores, stalls, and showrooms just across the river. Isle-sur-la-Sorgue is considered the antiques capital of the region, if not the country, and it's a good bet that many of the people who packed the town today were here for that reason alone.

After the big Sunday dinner we'd enjoyed, we chose to stay in for the evening and snack on cheese, bread, and wine.

Sunday dinner, Provence style

MONDAY, MAY 20

The Antiques Village

A lazy day. We had thoughts of getting in the car and driving to the nearby village of Ménerbes. We plan to visit a number of villages in the region while we're here, and Ménerbes seemed close enough to be a good destination for our first experience of driving in the Luberon. It then occurred to us that while Ménerbes would always be available, the antique stores wouldn't. They are open only Friday through Monday for what are enigmatically called "tax reasons." So we decided to stay local, tour the antiques village, and see what Isle was like without all the Sunday market-goers milling around.

We know next to nothing about antiques even at home, let alone in the south of France. So we decided to just take a quick spin through the 100-plus stores and stalls and see if anything caught our eye. A few things did, not because we wanted to buy them but because something about their style, or color, or size was noteworthy. It was fun.

The plan for a more in-depth tour of Isle basically flopped. Because the Sunday market deprives everyone of what would normally be a rest day, some people apparently move their sabbath rest to Monday, with the result that the town is largely closed for business. We will probably make a foray into the countryside tomorrow and then, God willing, get to see Isle up and running on Wednesday. We ate in for lunch, finishing the leftovers from yesterday's dinner, let ourselves snooze for a while in the afternoon, then sat out on our lovely balcony and did some reading.

Many of the town's restaurants, especially the higher-end ones, were closed so when dinnertime arrived the pickings were slim. One of the few available options was a bistro a few doors down named Au Cheneur. The food was unremarkable. For Peggy, a pork cutlet; for me a beefsteak that was generously portioned and cooked just right; for both of us a side of polenta and a pichet of a serviceable red house wine. The service, however, started out slightly distracted and soon devolved to inattentive. A number of what appeared to be regulars filtered in as the evening progressed and were taken care of promptly. We on the other hand had to flag down someone just to clear my plate. It wasn't a disaster by any means, just a step down from other dining experiences we've had on this trip.

Le Sentier des Ocres *(the Ochre Path) just outside Roussillon*

TUESDAY, MAY 21

On the Road: Roussillon and Gordes

Today was a gloriously sunny day and we were suffering a mild case of cabin fever, so we decided to hit the road.

Driving in Provence has its challenges. Except for a very few interstate-style divided highways, the roadways are either one or two lanes. Many of the two-lane roads are barely wide enough to warrant a stripe down the middle, and some of the one-lane roads are narrower than the typical hiking/biking path back home. The absence of shoulders in most places makes every encounter with an oncoming vehicle something of an adventure. Fortunately we haven't had any such encounters while driving the one-lane roads.

Speed limits—which reportedly are very strictly enforced—top out at 80 kph (50 mph), and only the natives have the nerve to actually go that fast. Most of the roads in the countryside are marked for 50 kph, those in town at 30 kph. The result is that it takes longer than you expect to get where you're trying to go. For example, although Ménerbes is only 18 kilometers from Isle (about 11 miles), the drive takes 30 minutes or more depending on traffic. Almost all road junctions feature roundabouts, some with as many as six or seven spokes. But they are well designed and well marked, and you get used to them quickly enough.

Our rental car is a Peugeot 3008 SUV. It is one of the nicest cars I've ever driven. If it were available in the U.S. it would move to the top of my list. GPS is available everywhere, and Peugeot's navigation system works well for the most part. Even so, it didn't take long to realize that Gwendolyn (my name for the navigation system voice—she's a Brit) has no qualms about directing us onto very skinny, truly scary roads. Once, she instructed me to turn onto a dirt two-track that ran through the middle of some farmer's field. I've learned that if I simply ignore her she quickly recalculates. At one point today I had to do this several times in a row before she came up with a routing that I considered reasonable.

• • •

Our first destination was Roussillon, a nearby village that gets a lot of love from guidebook writers, and deservedly so. France has semi-official lists of the "Most Beautiful" towns and villages in various regions. They are updated annually, and towns and villages make much of how many times they have been listed. Roussillon makes the list most years.

Roussillon's most distinctive feature is that it is in an area where red rock (ochre in this case) outcroppings are plentiful. It offers a walking tour through a nature area with particularly striking vistas, which is where we began the day. There was a 35-minute trail and a 55-minute trail. Being young and vibrant, we opted for the longer one. No regrets. There were some significant elevation changes, and many wooden steps with the inevitable coating of ochre dust, which made them treacherous for someone like me with knees in various stages of disintegration. Even so I will note that we completed the 55-minute trail in only 45 minutes.

After the hike we made a quick tour of the local cemetery, then went on to the town itself. It happens to be perched on the highest elevation in the area, creating wondrous views of the surrounding countryside. It is charming, with a lovely church, lots of traditional architecture, and a maze of streets and alleys.

We had lunch at the Bistrot de Roussillon, which offers a wonderful view of the countryside from its back terrace. The food was memorable. Peggy had the Salade du Bistrot, which featured fried *ravioles*. These are very small stuffed raviolis (barely a half-inch square), fried so as to serve the function normally filled by toasted croutons. I had the Cassolette de Ravioles, a baked dish featuring raviolis stuffed with cheese and topped with thin slices of parmesan and a lemon cream sauce. Irresistible.

We had passed the village of Gordes on the way to Roussillon and decided to stop there on the way home. Gordes is touted in all the guidebooks. According to one of them, it was essentially a ghost town in the 1960s when the newly launched Avignon Film Festival started bringing international film stars and studio moguls to Provence. They just *had* to have a "real" Provençal village of their very own, to serve both as a filming site and also as a suitable home for their kind of folk, so they essentially overhauled Gordes from top to bottom. The result is a village that looks spectacular, especially from a distance, but has few noteworthy sites.

I will remember our visit to Gordes as one of the more frustrating experiences of our trip. For one thing, it was windy. And I mean *windy*, as in strong, steady winds punctuated by gale-force gusts. At one point I took off my cap since there was no way to keep it on, and when I turned my head slightly my *sunglasses* blew off.

This phenomenon is known as the *Mistral* wind, and is the bane of life in Provence. It can be a brief episode, as in this case, or it can last for several days, forcing everyone indoors and bringing normal daily life to a standstill. The saving grace, the locals bravely say, is that it sweeps away the humidity, which accounts for the deep blue color of the sky and also prevents mildew in the vineyards. To the French, almost any hardship is tolerable if it makes the wine better. (I find no fault in this philosophy.)

The physical discomfort of the Mistral was only compounded by the near impossibility of navigating the town. Google Maps couldn't make heads or tails of the place, and when we finally found the *Office de Tourisme,* they provided a map which, so far as we could make out, did not seem to correspond to the place itself. It depicted streets that did not appear to exist, omitted the names of ones that did exist, and so on, and on, and on. When we finally realized that our long, unguided, hopelessly-lost peregrinations had led us, not just once but twice or even three times, along every street in the village with anything worth looking at, we went back to the car and let Gwendolyn lead us home, where wine and Four Roses bourbon awaited us.

Speaking of Four Roses: It was a venerable U.S. label that was bought by the Seagrams company and, in the late 1950s, assigned exclusively to the European and Asian markets. It was reintroduced in the States in 2002. It's still quite popular in Europe—indeed, in many places we visited it was the only brand other than Jack Daniels that was available.

• • •

Back in Isle, we dropped in for dinner at La Praline, a nice *crêperie* with distinctive green awnings that we can see from our balcony. We shared a plate of assorted cheeses, meats, vegetables, and tapenades, and a pichet of Rosé. We knew before we arrived that Rosé was a very big deal in Provence, and we've made a point of trying it out. In the U.S., Rosé has sometimes been scorned as something the winemaker has concocted from sub-par or leftover reds and whites. In Provence it is recognized, indeed celebrated, as a category unto itself, and is the primary focus of a great many winemakers. We have already encountered a number of excellent Rosés with distinctive colors, bouquets, and flavors. They would work wonderfully in situations where one might otherwise choose a white or a sparkling wine.

THE MAN WITH THE BAGUETTE

Café de France: "our" café in Isle

WEDNESDAY, MAY 22

Jouets, Poupées, and a Change in Plans

Today was to be, at last, the day for us to see Isle-sur-la-Sorgue operating at full capacity. But it turns out that many shops and restaurants close on Wednesdays, for reasons unknown to me. Commerce in Provence really does march to a different drummer. This relaxed rhythm would undoubtedly make life in Provence more serene. It's just a little puzzling for newcomers.

We did visit the town's only museum, the Musée de Jouets et de les Poupées Ancien. (*Jouet* means toy, and *poupée* means doll.) It originally consisted of one woman's private doll collection, which has been supplemented by many additions over the years. It is a marvelously eclectic conglomeration of genuine treasures and more than a little kitsch. We had the privilege of being escorted through the galleries by two charming elderly ladies, whose passion for the collection is unmistakable. They didn't speak English but I was able to roughly translate at least some of what they told us. One of those things was that the museum will be closing for good in October. *Quelle dommage.*

We had lunch at the venerable Café de France, on the square beside the church. A nice salad and a good Rosé under a bright sun in a cloudless sky. Life is good.

• • •

Much of the day was taken up with mundane concerns. I woke up at 4:00am gripped by worry that our rental car, which I had parked in a lot behind the Post Office, might have been be ticketed or towed. When the sun came up I got dressed and set forth on a mission to move the car to a safer place. An hour later, having gotten myself hopelessly lost in spite of Gwendolyn's best efforts, I finally found a free public lot near the train station. I later learned that my worries were unfounded: the lot behind the Post Office was also free, just not clearly marked as such.

Later in the day we decided to completely revamp our plan for getting back home at the end of the trip (still almost two weeks away). That plan had us driving from Isle to Marseilles on Monday, spending the night at the airport, and then flying from Marseilles to Paris on Tuesday morning to connect with our flight home. The problem was that there was barely an hour between our scheduled arrival from Marseilles and our scheduled departure from Paris, which felt too close for comfort.

We decided we would skip Marseilles altogether, instead take a high-speed train from Avignon directly to CDG on Monday and spend the night there, then catch our flight home on Tuesday. A couple hours later, after fruitless visits to the local train station and a local travel agency, not to mention fighting through endlessly repeating telephone loops with both Delta and Air France, followed by an infuriating circular feedback loop on the web site for OUIGO, France's low-cost train system, all the pieces were in place. We were aided in this endeavor by our stateside travel agent, Myrna, who later told us she had been horrified by the very idea of rearranging a long-established itinerary on the fly. I guess all's well that ends well.

• • •

We had a terrific dinner at La Balade de Saveurs (which I would loosely render as "Parade of Flavors"), a very nice restaurant with seating alongside the Sorgue. The appetizer was a terrine of duck that completed my conversion into a lover of terrine. Peggy had a main course consisting of the most tender veal steak imaginable, served with flawlessly prepared vegetables. I had poached sea bass on a bed of savory black rice. All accompanied by a bottle of Bandol, a wonderful red wine featuring the Mourvèdre grape. There will definitely be more of that grape in our future. For dessert, a delicate chocolate mousse on a crust made of coconut. Excellent in every respect.

Ménerbes became our favorite village in the Luberon.

THURSDAY, MAY 23

Road Trip: Ménerbes and Lacoste

Another beautiful day. The forecast was for a high of 80°F and it got there. I was emboldened to wear shorts for the first time on the trip and am glad I did.

Today was to be a tour of three Luberon villages: Ménerbes, Lacoste, and Bonnieux. None of these has any marquee sights or monuments, and as a result many guidebooks have little to say about them. It is the villages themselves, the views of the surrounding area, and their relaxed pace of life that are the attraction.

• • •

Ménerbes was *superbe*. It enjoys a picturesque setting high atop one of the larger hills in the area. The village itself is lovely, with the by-now familiar labyrinth of narrow streets, very few cars, and very small crowds. Today was market day, which depending on what you're after might seem to be a good reason for staying away. But the Ménerbes market was quite small and located on the outskirts and didn't impinge on the village much at all.

Ménerbes was the village near which the British author Peter Mayle lived when he wrote his well-loved book *A Year in Provence* and its sequels. His celebrity turned Ménerbes into a prominent tourist attraction about 35 years ago, with attendant crowds, noise, and high prices. Indeed, Mayle moved to New York in 1996 to escape all the fuss he himself had created. Ménerbes has long since recaptured its native charm, though the positive economic impact of that era still shows itself in the village's well-groomed buildings and nicely-paved streets.

We took a lot of pictures of those streets and buildings, of the spectacular views of the farms, fields, and houses that lay in the valley below, and of the Petit Luberon and Great Luberon mountain ranges in the distance. The highest peak is Mont Ventoux, which can be seen from miles away in all directions thanks to the clear Provence air. But mostly we just moseyed along, breathed deeply, and felt our pulse rates and blood pressures go down. After a snack at a café called Chez Auzet, we reluctantly left Ménerbes and set off for our next stop.

• • •

That next stop was Lacoste, a smaller village atop a smaller hill, with an unusual set of cultural pedigrees. Its place in history owes to the fact that the Marquis de Sade built a castle in town and lived there for 30 years, doing the things that ultimately made him infamous and got him arrested. Today the town appears to owe its livelihood to the Savannah College of Art and Design (SCAD), in which are enrolled students from many countries, primarily the U.S. It is oddly disconcerting to drive a narrow winding road up the side of a mountain in the south of France, then walk narrow winding paths further up the side of the mountain in search of the proverbial village that time forgot, and suddenly find yourself in the midst of what feels rather like a small American college town.

Lacoste can of course be represented on conventional two-dimensional maps, but you really need the third dimension to understand what it takes to get from here to there. The operative question regarding any proposed destination is not "how far is it" but "how far *up* is it." Peggy and I climbed (that is precisely the word) from the central square past the Portail de la Garde (historically an important part of the village's defenses) to the SCAD, and then up, up, and *way* up to the Chateau de Lacoste, the town's signature attraction, an ancient castle that stands at the tippy-top of the mountain. All this by means of narrow, winding, *steep* streets made of cobblestone. Of course what goes up must come down, in this case via the same route, which was almost as challenging on the descent as on the ascent. For all that, we liked Lacoste. It has a stern beauty that contrasts nicely with the more genteel Ménerbes.

We dutifully made the drive to nearby Bonnieux, which looks impressive from a distance but has little to offer once you get there. It is in fact not a village but a decent-sized town, with stoplights, crosswalks, and its own local bus service. We drove through it but couldn't work up any enthusiasm to get out and walk around. In fairness to Bonnieux, our judgment was certainly influenced by the degree to which we had been enchanted by Ménerbes and exhausted by Lacoste. In any event we turned around and drove back to Isle-sur-la-Sorgue.

• • •

This evening we enjoyed a light dinner at Café de France. Even the hamburgers in Provence are culinary delights.

• • •

We made today's excursion without the full benefit of the car's navigation system, which for reasons unfathomable seemed to be missing half of its functionality. Driving in Provence is sufficiently confusing that you want all the navigation functionality you can get. It just so happened that there was a licensed Peugeot repair shop down the street from our apartment, and we stopped there on our way home. What ensued was a hilarious episode in which I tried to describe the problem to the chief mechanic, who had no English, through the intermediation of the shop's receptionist, who had not much more. We ended up in a Rube Goldberg-like communications loop: I would describe something to the receptionist in fractured Franglish, and when we reached impasse she would sit me down at her computer so I could use Google Translate. She would then try to describe the situation in French to the mechanic, who inevitably had follow-up questions that she couldn't readily convey to me in English and that I probably couldn't have answered anyway. But all ended well. The mechanic silently demonstrated the process of programming the system, and I *think* I followed it all. Anyway, the system returned to full functionality.

*The French have a saying: "The worse the soil, the better the wine."
If that's true, these vines should produce very good wine indeed.*

FRIDAY, MAY 24

Terroirs of the Rhône

Today we took a marvelous wine tour with Olivier Hackman, a British expat who moved to France some years ago. He was a wine geek who left his accountant job in London, invested considerable effort in researching the wines of the Rhône district (Côtes du Rhône, Gigondas, and Châteauneuf du Pape among others) and now offers day-long tours in which he teaches about *terroir*, both in general terms and also as it applies to the wines of this region. We took a morning train into Avignon and met him at the Hotel L'Horloge. Also on the tour were an older couple from New Orleans and a younger couple from New York. We all squeezed into Olivier's small van and off we went.

During the drive north Olivier delivered his discourse. It was extremely informative and thoroughly entertaining. Highlights included:

- The *terroir* of each individual plot of ground is unique. Not just the soil itself but the complete natural environment in which the grapes grow, including wind, temperature, slope, etc.

- The growers are not interested in creating or replicating a particular taste year after year but in capturing and expressing the *terroir* of the moment. They take it for granted that a bottle drawn from grapes grown in one location may taste different than a bottle drawn from grapes grown only a short distance away.

- The growers are extremely resistant to employing any outside agent in the process. The grapes grow as nature and circumstances dictate, without irrigation, and ferment on their own, according to their particular composition, without added yeast or any other "artificial" ingredients or human intervention.

• They refer to themselves as "wine *growers*," not "wine *makers*," as the latter implies a level of human manipulation of the process that they disdain.

• There are different levels of appellations for wine, each with its own standards that are closely monitored by the authorities. For starters, wines in this region are classified by geography, not by varietal, and may not be identified by any geographic appellation unless all the grapes come from that particular area. In this region there are three levels of appellations: Côtes du Rhône; Côtes du Rhone Villages; and Cru. Other regions have additional layers such Grand Cru or Premiere Cru. When asked whether the granting of appellations was political, Olivier replied, tongue firmly in cheek, "Political? In France? Who could imagine anything in France being influenced by politics?"

• The saying is that the harsher the growing conditions, the better the wine. The more sand, clay, and rocks the better, as this "stresses" the vine, forcing it to drive its roots deeper, often as far as 40 feet. The use of irrigation short-circuits this process, resulting in lesser-quality wines.

• Wine is typically aged in concrete vats. Oak barrels are used only in specialized circumstances as the wine growers generally do not want any oak taste. Even then they use very large barrels as this minimizes the grapes' contact with the oak.

• As a rule the French do not drink wine by itself, but take it only with food. When they are tasting wines they tend to talk, not in terms of the nose, the aftertaste, and so on, but in terms of what foods would be complemented by it. Thus instead of "I'm getting hints of leather and apricots," they will say, "I would serve this with…"

- The Mistral wind is indispensable in growing grapes here as it drives out humidity and prevents mildew. People who live here and have to contend with the Mistral try to console themselves with this knowledge.

- Most wines from this region are blends of three grapes: Grenache (primarily), Syrah, and Mourvèdre, though of course some are drawn from a single grape. The specific grapes and their proportions are not identified on the label, though almost every other conceivable piece of information is listed there.

• • •

We visited four *vignobles* (vineyards). The first was Domaine Bressy-Masson, in Rasteau, a lesser-known appellation. We had planned to buy one bottle at each stop, with some preference given to wines we won't be able to find back home. Here we selected a *Rasteau Cuvée Paul Emile* 2016. In keeping with our previous finding that very good wines are available for very low prices in France, it cost only €16.

Second was Domaine la Fourmone near Vacqueyras and Gigondas. We bought a *Vacqueyras Ceps d'Or* 2012. We had also tasted the 2015 vintage of the same wine, and the extra three years of aging made a noticeable difference. Cost was about €15.

Third was the nearby Domaine la Garrigue. Here we enjoyed a wonderful four-course *déjeunais* with wine pairings. It was a perfect Provençal day in a beautiful location with great food and wine. We bought their Gigondas 2016 (about €15).

The final stop was Domaine Font de Michelle, near the town of Châteauneuf du Pape. We began with a visit to one of their vineyards, where we had a chance to see at first hand the "soil" in which the grapes that make up this type of wine (mainly Grenache) are grown. It consists of a top layer of rocks—not little stones, but fist-sized rocks—with a sand underlay. If Olivier's maxim is true, that the worst soil makes the best wine, this setting promises very fine wine indeed.

We then visited the winery itself, where we got a tour from one of the owners followed by a tasting. We sampled five wines, each one better than the one before. We liked all of them, and loved a couple of them, but were really blown away by a late addition to the lineup, a Châteauneuf du Pape called *Élégance de Jeanne*. It cost €50, and sells for roughly $90 in the U.S. (all of this vineyard's wines are available here).

• • •

The drive back to the Avignon Centre train station was short in kilometers but incredibly slow, owing to traffic and road construction around the city. We were just able to catch the 5:47 train for the short run back to Isle. After an exhilarating-but-exhausting day, and in the wake of the splendid lunch we had enjoyed, we were more than content to stay in for a cheese/viande/olive/bread snack-dinner and an early bedtime.

Le Prévôté

SATURDAY, MAY 25

Le Prévôté

After a long day yesterday we were happy to kick back and relax this morning. It was yet another in a long string of picture-perfect days. We had lunch at Grand Café de la Sorgue, just around the corner from us, along the riverbank. I was happy to see that the lunch menu was a departure from the usual, with many standby dishes missing and many intriguing new ones included. We shared a tuna salad (a description that doesn't begin to do it justice) and a pichet of Rosé. I'd like to check it out for dinner sometime. After lunch we took a long stroll through the town, dropping into many shops we hadn't previously been able to visit.

• • •

This evening was one of the most anticipated events of the trip. Last Christmas our kids gave us a special "gift card." They had done their research and identified the best place to have dinner in Isle: a gourmet restaurant named Le Prévôté. (It is also a high-end hotel.) It is located on an obscure lane not far from the church. We went looking for it earlier in the week and it took us a while to find it, even with the help of Google Maps.

Le Prévôté is unprepossessing from the outside but charming on the inside. When we passed through the main gate we found ourselves in a small courtyard. The entrances to the restaurant and hotel were side by side. Only when we were inside could we discover that the building was erected directly over a small tributary of the Sorgue. The lobbies had glass flooring to display this feature.

The interior of the restaurant was elegant but not ostentatious. Similarly the wait staff was congenial and efficient and not the least bit stuffy. And the food! From a very sumptuous menu we selected a *prix-fixe* dinner with seven courses (I think—it was hard to keep track) and three flights of wine selected by the sommelier to complement the food. We were so charmed by the setting, and so engrossed in the food and wine, that we completely forgot to write down what we had. But it was all wonderful.

This is definitely a place where the table is yours for the evening. The staff waited until it was clear that both of us had finished one course before clearing and re-setting the table. The pace of delivering the various courses was relaxed, as were we by the end of the meal.

One of the things that has made dining out so enjoyable on this trip is that all the restaurants we've visited have been within walking distance of our apartments. Nothing complements a great meal better than being able to get up from the table and casually walk home. That is especially true here in Provence where there is no city noise or traffic to deal with.

Jazzman extraordinaire *Leonard Blair*

SUNDAY, MAY 26

Leonard

Today is *Fête Maman* (Mother's Day) in France. The holiday was duly noted at mass this morning, though it was not the main event. The stars of today's show were ten children making their First Communion. They processed in with the priest, all dressed in white. This ran the gamut from a young lady in a dress that could almost serve as a wedding gown, to a little boy wearing white shorts and white sneakers. But the First Communion wasn't all: two of the children also got baptized and confirmed. Sacramental Bonanza! Liturgical Extravaganza! For all this, it was pretty much like First Communions everywhere: the priest, who was clearly well acquainted with the children, posing questions to them individually during the homily; the Litany of the Saints *(all* of the Saints); the lighting of candles, and so on. At the end of mass the children were presented with gift bags from the church. I have no idea what was in them.

Last Sunday was rainy, so we figured we'd have a better time doing the Sunday Market today. It was pretty much the same as last week, though it seemed that there were more clothing stands and fewer meat/cheese/produce stands. I bought a cap which, with any luck, might make me appear a little less obviously American. We wandered around for a while, then noticed that many of the food stands were almost empty, and merchants were packing to go home. We had gotten a late start because of the length of the mass. We made a beeline to the stand where we bought the roasted chicken last week; we also bought asparagus, tomatoes, strawberries, almonds, cheeses, and of course a baguette, with which to repeat our now-traditional Provençal Sunday Dinner.

Among the highlights of the Isle markets are musicians who perform in various locations. As I write this, just below our balcony is a saxophonist/singer named Leonard Blair who, we are told, sets up at this location and at this time every Sunday afternoon. His repertoire is American jazz standards, and he is an excellent performer. So: on a picture-perfect Sunday afternoon I am sitting on the balcony of our small Provençal apartment, writing my reflections about our time in France, sipping a nice Viogner, and being serenaded by Leonard. I don't see how it gets any better than this. I already know exactly where I will be next Sunday afternoon from 4:00 to 6:00pm: right where I am now.

Roman Amphithéâtre, Arles. Like the neighboring Théâtre Classique, it is two centuries old and still in use today.

MONDAY, MAY 27

Arles, Les Baux, and St-Rémy

Today we once again put on our travelin' shoes. The admittedly ambitious plan was to drive to Arles, then to Les Baux-de-Provence, and finally to St-Rémy. Construction delays and a recurrence of last week's navigation problems made the one-hour drive to Arles take almost two hours. We stopped along the way at an office of our car-rental agency, EuropCar, where the man slowly walked us through the somewhat non-intuitive French method of programming the system. Peggy watched intently and caught a step in the process that neither of us had noticed at our previous demonstration in Isle. Mystery solved at last! Even so, when we left Arles for Les Baux, Gwendolyn inexplicably steered us toward Avignon, many miles out of our way. We doubled back and eventually got to our intended destination. The various glitches cost us almost two hours.

• • •

Arles is a nice town, a good home base for sightseeing in the southwest part of Provence. Vincent Van Gogh lived in Arles for a time, including a stretch in a sanitarium, and painted many well-known works here. But none of those works (nor any other Van Gogh paintings, so far as I can tell) is actually housed in Arles. Many other cities, not only in France but throughout Europe, strain to exploit any conceivable Van Gogh connection; in Arles this includes placing plaques at spots where he is thought to have set up his easel for some of his paintings. This is not especially satisfying. For example, the plaque for the famous painting of "the yellow house" stands in the midst of what is now a crowded public square filled with cafés and souvenir shops, the yellow house itself having disappeared long ago.

We spent some quality time at two of Arles's best-known, and most photogenic, attractions: the Amphithéâtre and the Théâtre Classique, both Roman ruins that are centuries old but still in use today.

• • •

Les Baux-de-Provence is home to the aptly named Chateau Des Baux, the ancient ruins of an enormous stone castle perched atop a hill with commanding views of the countryside in all directions. The ruins are amazing in themselves: massive structures that have eroded over the centuries but remain imposing today. What is truly remarkable, however, is to try to imagine how immense this castle must have been in its day, and what must have gone into its construction. Its highest lookouts and parapets remain, still reachable in part by sections of the original stairways. Only in Europe, with its casual approach to personal and public safety (not to mention the absence of a tort law system), would it be thinkable to let tourists climb these steps. Even so, when confronted with the scariest-looking climb of all, to the highest lookout of all, Peggy was game, so up we went. Our efforts were rewarded with spectacular views of the surrounding area, which included similar stone ruins on one side and farm country on the other side stretching for miles before reaching the foothills of the Luberon mountains in the distance.

• • •

We took a well-known scenic loop from Les Baux to St-Rémy and back again (D-5 down, D-27 back). St-Rémy is a well-groomed town with lots of tony shops, trendy restaurants, and chic hotels. It would be a good, if somewhat pricey, home base for sightseeing. Its centrally-located Old Town, however, is little different from similar districts in other cities. We had thought of finding dinner here, but in light of the overlong travel and unusually strenuous activity we had already experienced, we decided it made more sense to get back to Isle before dark and have dinner there.

About that dinner, the less said the better. Suffice to say that our entry in the Eva's guest book will advise future visitors to opt for dining at establishments other than Le Quai des Bouchons.

The Sorgue River as it flows through le bassin *(basin) at the eastern end of Isle-sur-la-Sorgue*

TUESDAY, MAY 28

Fontaine-de-Vaucluse

After yesterday's long drive and tour of old ruins we slept late, relaxed and drank coffee all morning, walked to the *Poste* to mail postcards to the kids, and then wandered the streets of Isle, mostly checking out various restaurants and which days they are open.

By mid-afternoon we were feeling restless and decided to visit Fontaine-de-Vaucluse, where the Sorgue has its source. It is said that the source is only visibly active in the early spring when the winter snow melts; the rest of the year there is nothing to be seen. We envisioned a short drive to the village, a brief stroll to see the currently-non-flowing source of the river, then home-again, home-again, jiggety-jig.

It didn't work out that way. There were sizable crowds. Their impact was compounded by enormous motor coaches, filled with school children or senior citizens as the case might be, stopped in the middle of the only road into town, blocking traffic in both directions. Once these were cleared it quickly became apparent that there was not a single parking spot to be had anywhere in the Greater Fontaine-de-Vaucluse Metropolitan Area. After much wailing and gnashing of teeth we finally instructed Gwendoline to point the way back home.

We had dinner at Le Carré d'Herbes, a quaint restaurant tucked into a corner of the antiques village, which had been recommended to us by another restaurateur. Everything was wonderful. Peggy had chicken breast stuffed with chèvre and kale, and I had sea bream, all complemented by a delicious Ventoux wine called *À mon père*.

Le Palais des Papes

WEDNESDAY, MAY 29

Avignon: the Palace and the Bridge

We got touristy today and decided to tour Avignon because...well, because you're *supposed* to tour Avignon when you're in this part of France. Having seen how godawful the traffic and parking in Avignon could be when we were there last Friday for the wine tour, we decided to go by train. It is so nice to be in a world where reliable train service is readily available. And cheap: our round-trip tickets cost only €3,90 each.

We went first to Avignon's signature attraction, the Palais des Papes. They do a remarkably good job of making the place interesting. The fact is that a tour of the palace is basically a long trek through a number of large rooms, most of which are completely empty and offer nothing substantive to look at. Many times when a room *does* have something to look at, it's behind glass or a rope or whatever.

What saves the day is a device called the Histo-Pod (history + iPod?). It is a small tablet that hangs around your neck and provides computer-generated visuals of what the room you are currently in looked like (or might have looked like) in the 14th century. You can point it at any part of the room—including the floors and ceilings—or do a 360-degree pan, and the Histo-Pod brings it to life. It is infinitely preferable to simply listening to an audio guide droning on about things you cannot see.

After that we went to the Pont St-Bénézet, better known as the famous Pont D'Avignon where, in the old children's song, one dances *tous en rond* (all in a circle). One slightly cuckoo element of the tour was the chance to listen to the old ditty being performed—by computer—in eight different musical styles including "country," "bossa nova," and—my favorite—"acid jazz." (I'd never heard of it, either.)

Work on the bridge was started in the 12th century but was never completed. It extends about halfway across the Rhine and then simply stops (the *real* "bridge to nowhere"). Some excellent audio-visual programs explain how bridges like this were built back then, which was an astounding engineering feat. We walked a little way out onto the bridge itself, but between the overpowering Mistral wind that rose up today and my phobia of exposed heights (more on that in a moment), we didn't get very far.

There is also a tour. The inevitable audio guide tells more than you really need to know about St. Bénézet himself, who was not actually a saint at all, but a shepherd boy lionized by the local populace for having performed heroic feats which, so far as anyone has been able to determine, never actually took place.

There are lots of other interesting sights in Avignon, many of which we walked by and took pictures of, but none that we wanted to spend much time or energy on. We ate lunch at one of the dozens of cafés that fill the central Place de L'Horloge, then caught our return train.

• • •

Dinner tonight at El Nego, a nice restaurant along the river. We sat inside because we'd had enough of being pummeled by the wind, which was still up at this hour. I decided try out an entrée with escargots. It tasted a lot like cream of mushroom soup except that the cream was much better and the escargots were bigger, tastier, and chewier. I had a risotto and whitefish main course and Peggy had skewered lamb. Both were delicious, as was the Ventoux wine.

Les Terraces, a picturesque restaurant alongside le bassin

THURSDAY, MAY 30

The Other Market Day

As before on days following a strenuous sightseeing adventure, we took today as a rest day in Isle.

Thursday is the "other" market day here. The Thursday market is indeed smaller than the Sunday one—only about half as much area is set aside for it, and it ends earlier in the afternoon—but it is still bigger than most of the markets in the surrounding villages.

It was yet another perfect day. We wandered around the market and eventually bought a sandwich for a picnic on our balcony, which was our front-row seat to another performance by our new friend Leonard. I went down and made a request (*Do You Know What It Means to Miss New Orleans?*), which he played, and then chatted with him. He is originally from New Orleans but now lives here in Isle. He fronts a trio called Gig Street, which performs in the area and occasionally ventures farther afield. They once performed in Ann Arbor and then in East Lansing, as part of what Leonard called "my work with Xavier University." I bought one of his CDs, and we are now friends on Facebook. I plan to be on the balcony when he sets up here again this Sunday.

A little later in the afternoon Peggy and I went for a walk, focusing on segments of the antiques village we hadn't seen before. Among other activities, we bought a bottle of Ventoux wine that we enjoyed back at the apartment this evening.

• • •

We had dinner at Les Terraces, easily the most picturesque restaurant in town. It sits along the *bassin* at the east end of the island, where the

Sorgue splits in two and makes its way past spectacular gardens and over man-made waterfalls. The restaurant's riverside terraces and tables are draped with long white cloths that billow in the breeze. We shared an entrée of roasted pepper stuffed with chèvre that was very nice. Peggy's main course was a grilled giant shrimp—almost the size of a lobster tail—that was excellent. I ordered entrecôte, which was so-so. Veal and lamb have consistently been good choices wherever we've gone on this trip, and fish and seafood have been consistently excellent. But I've found that beef can be iffy in France. Mine was undercooked, though to the chef's credit, when I sent it back they didn't go overboard and bring it back well-done, as often happens. All that said, we had a nice evening in a beautiful setting in Provence. Can't complain about that.

Chapelle de l'Annonciade, Crestet

FRIDAY, MAY 31

Mont Ventoux, Wines of the Côtes du Rhône

When we set out on our final major excursion, the idea was to take a driving tour of Côtes du Rhône wineries laid out in one of the guidebooks. We noticed that the itinerary would bring us near Mont Ventoux. At roughly 6,300 feet (1919 meters), Mont Ventoux is the highest point in the region. For reference, Pike's Peak is 14,000 feet. But for this part of the world, Mont Ventoux is a beast. The ascent of Mont Ventoux is the most difficult and most famous leg of the annual Tour de France, making it catnip for serious cyclists everywhere, who flock to it in droves (as do many casual riders). We hadn't planned on driving it, but there it was, so…

• • •

Route D-974 is one of those not-quite-two-lane roads that snakes and switchbacks its way up the western face of the mountain. Every inch of it is on a razor's edge. There are no shoulders on either side, nor any guardrails, so the outboard side of the road simply drops off into the ever-deepening abyss. They tell me there are spectacular views on this drive. I wouldn't know because, by sheer force of will, I never looked at them. "Never" as in not once, even for a moment. My phobia of exposed heights is slightly ameliorated by being enclosed in a vehicle, but only very slightly. I was honestly afraid that if I so much as peeked, I might go woozy or even pass out.

Every so often, of course, we would encounter a vehicle coming *down* the mountain, requiring a delicate *pas-de-deux* by both drivers, neither of whom had much margin for error. To make matters still worse, the entire route was crawling with packs of the aforementioned cyclists. I don't think it is an exaggeration to say that there were more than a thousand of them on the mountain that morning. Needless to say, there was no such thing as a "bike lane," which meant that in order to get around the cyclists, vehicles ascending the mountain had to borrow some of the real estate belonging to the vehicles descending the mountain. Imagine making that maneuver as you approach a switchback with no way of knowing whether you might be about to encounter a vehicle coming the other way.

I was a nervous wreck the whole way. Peggy was in the even more unnerving position of being powerless to affect anything that was happening. I could tell she was using all her strength not to show her concern lest it distract me from my driving. I freely admit that I would have gladly turned back at any point along the way but for the fact that there was never a single reasonable opportunity to do so.

We were a lovely pair of basket cases when we finally reached the summit—where we discovered that there was not a single square inch of space to even stop the car, let alone get out and enjoy the presumably spectacular vistas we had won at such cost. Nothing to be done but to immediately head down the southern face of the mountain on D-974. This second leg of the trip was only slightly less terrifying than the first, because the ascending cyclists were now someone else's problem.

• • •

When we finally reached the bottom of Mont Ventoux we renewed our wine road tour. We stopped in a tiny village called Crestet, which according to the guidebooks was known for its one, single, solitary restaurant, where the food was so-so but the views were spectacular. We made our way up to the village and picked our way through the narrow streets, only to discover that the restaurant was closed for a major renovation.

The saving grace was that Crestet was one of the most charming villages we have seen.

Next stop was Vaison-la-Romaine, a fairly large town with a "medieval village" perched atop a neighboring hill. There wasn't a lot to see there, but there were a number of restaurants that we spotted on the way in and planned to patronize on the way out. This would have been a good plan but for the fact that all of said establishments closed their kitchens at precisely 2:00pm and had no sympathy for those, like us, who arrived at 2:02pm. We ended up getting lousy salads at a forgettable tourist-trap crêperie at the bottom. (Hey, not *all* the meals can be culinary masterpieces.)

We had planned next to visit a well-known winery somewhere in the vicinity of the town of Séguret. Our guidebook did a masterful job of telling us how hard the winery was to find, but offered no help in actually finding it. This led to several false starts and backtracks. We were ready to throw in the towel when we came upon a local who knew the winery and gave us directions. We decided to give it one last try.

We were glad we did when we finally arrived at Domaine de Mourchon. Not surprisingly, given how hard it is to find the place, we were the only people in the tasting room and had the undivided attention of Walter, the Scotsman who founded and still runs the winery, and his assistant Laurie. Their wines were wonderful. We bought a bottle to take home with us and picked up an order form for an incredible deal whereby we can place an order that will be fulfilled by the winery's U.S. distributor in Chicago, for essentially the same price as if we'd bought it on the spot. The only drawback is that they will not ship wines during hot weather, i.e., summer. So we will have to remember to place an order in October.

• • •

Isle seemed unusually crowded when we returned from the day's adventures. We had learned that yesterday had been a "bank holiday," and that many people also took off work on Friday to create a four-day weekend. From the level of activity in the town, and the level of noise and commotion below our balcony, we were afraid we might find ourselves trapped in a raucous holiday weekend. But by 7:00pm everything had calmed down, as always.

We had a wonderful dinner at Café le France. The weather was perfect, the food and drink were simple but exquisite, and we enjoyed the kind of long, lingering evening that one dreams of when thinking of France, gazing up through the plane trees at the church spire overlooking the square.

View from Bistrot le 5, Ménerbes

SATURDAY, JUNE 1

Return to Ménerbes

One nice aspect of staying in the same place for two weeks is that if you go someplace or do something that you really enjoy, and you're thinking to yourself, "I'd really love to do that again someday," you can.

This explains how we came to spend today revisiting Ménerbes, our favorite of all the villages we've visited. We've concluded it could be a good spot for a longer visit. It doesn't have nearly the range of shops and restaurants that Isle has right on your doorstep. But it has enough of them that you could spend a delightful, serene week there without having to get in the car every time you need something. At the same time it is small and non-commercial enough that even its market day is peaceful and quiet.

When we were in Ménerbes last week we noticed a restaurant called Bistrot le 5, with a great location on the hillside and dozens of outdoor tables from which to enjoy a beautiful view. It opens for lunch every day but Monday. It's also open for dinner on Friday and Saturday but I didn't want to drive home in the dark. So we made a reservation for lunch today.

And what a lunch it was. We started with Gros Escargots de Bourgogne (big snails Burgundy-style). Being newbies, we had to ask the server to demonstrate how to eat them. You get a special pair of tongs for holding the shell in place and a small two-tined fork with which to dig the meat out of the shell. We eventually got the hang of it. It was fun, and the escargots were wonderful.

For our main courses, Peggy had baked salmon and I had a seven-hour-cooked lamb shoulder so tender that the meat all but fell off the bone. Both were among the most delicious dishes we've tasted in France.

Sitting out on a terrace on a beautiful day, looking out over the countryside with a delightful Provençal Rosé, only made it better.

We have noticed throughout this trip that the French are really into dessert. In U.S. restaurants the servers typically go through the motions of offering it and are somewhat startled if anyone accepts. Not so in France. Lots of desserts are served with lunches and dinners, along with lots of coffee. We decided to invoke the when-in-Rome principle and shared a *crème brûlée* along with two *café crèmes*.

• • •

On the way home we decided to stop at Domaine de la Citadelle, a winery just outside Ménerbes. It is known as the home of the Musée du Tire-Bouchons ("pull-stoppers"): the Museum of Corkscrews. They have more than 1200 corkscrews, from many different countries, some going back hundreds of years. It sounds like it might be France's answer to The World's Biggest Ball of Twine, but in fact there have a been number of different types of devices used in different places at different times. It only took about twenty minutes to walk through it but it was interesting.

The winery also has an extensive botanical garden where they grow hundreds of different types of herbs and other plants. It spreads across five terraces that rise up the hill behind the main house. Peggy, who plants a small herb garden every year, was in awe of the variety. All in all it made for a very pleasant, not-too-strenuous day in the outdoors.

• • •

No way could we handle a full dinner after that lunch. We stayed home, sat out on our balcony, took a leisurely stroll around town, nibbled on some of the cheese and meats that have accumulated in our refrigerator, and worked on depleting our wine inventory to a size we can take home on the plane. Perfect evening.

Last dinner in Provence

SUNDAY, JUNE 2

Café Fleurs

It had to come: last day in Provence. Last deep-deep-deep blue sky. Last cappuccino by the Sorgue. Last time through the Sunday market, where we bought prints of paintings of Isle and Ménerbes as mementos. Last jazz set from Leonard below our balcony. Last Aperol Spritz at our favorite local spot, the Café de France. Last dinner in Provence.

For this we chose Café Fleurs, which had come highly recommended and did not disappoint. Entrées of assorted heirloom tomatoes with fresh burrata cheese and pearls of balsamic vinegar for Peggy; grilled salmon and crispy prawns for me. Main courses of baked cod on a bed of parmesan risotto with broccolini and snow peas for Peggy; duck breast with a delicate and blessedly non-sticky-sweet sauce, plus duck confit within a breaded "purse" for me. Desserts of astonishingly flavorful *glaces* for both of us. All accompanied by a delicious red wine from Domaine de Lauziéres, in Les Baux-de-Provence, called *Equinox*. The crowning touch was that our orders were taken, our dishes served, and our wine poured by the chef himself, Yvon Morgan.

The apartment in Isle-sur-la-Sorgue

MONDAY, JUNE 3

Homeward Bound, Day 1

After two weeks in Isle-sur-la-Sorgue we feel much as our friend Myrna did about both the town and the apartment: it's awfully hard to say goodbye. The town is an ideal base for touring, and the apartment an ideal place to experience life in Provence.

Isle offered everything we could have asked for, all within easy walking distance—restaurants, groceries, wine shops, you name it. The apartment was delightful. Like the Paris apartment, this one had a wonderful combination of traditional construction and modern appliances and conveniences, not to mention the balcony where we spent many restful hours, and our host, Eva, made sure we had everything we needed. The apartment also had delightful quirks. The bedroom was a half-storey lower than the rest of the apartment (the same was true of the second bedroom in Paris), and was reached by a rather steep, curved stairway with a "banister" made of a thick manila rope. This added a dash of excitement to things.

• • •

We did such a good job of organizing things yesterday that we were packed and ready to go long before Eva was due to arrive to see us off and reclaim the apartment keys. So we went for a short walk through the village, passing what have become familiar landmarks.

Before we closed the suitcases for the last time, I stopped in at a gift shop across the street to pick up a souvenir: a small ceramic *cigalle* (cicada). We saw these almost everywhere we went in Provence, including a rather large one in our apartment. Despite being ugly, cicadas are beloved in Provence because they signal the arrival of summer, when they chirp nonstop from sunup to sundown. Our little yellow *cigalle* will be a nice memento of our time here.

We got in the car and drove away at about 1:30. We fueled up in Isle—amazingly, a single tank of *gazole* (diesel fuel) had been sufficient for our entire two-week visit—and set out for Avignon. Notwithstanding that I had carefully entered the precise address for the rental car office, Gwendolyn—no doubt as a parting gesture—led us to a distant corner of the train station's long-term parking area. We eventually found our way to the Europcar office and returned the Peugeot without incident. As wonderful as it was to be able to drive ourselves around Provence in comfort, it was a relief to be rid of responsibility for the car. I had accustomed myself to many of the quirks of driving in France, but even so, when we entered the Avignon area this afternoon it felt good to be back on an ordinary street grid with normal-width lanes and stoplights.

Unlike airports, train stations are not designed with the thought in mind that passengers might need to spend a bit of time in them. This is certainly true of Avignon TGV. It offers only a couple gift and food shops, and almost nothing in the way of comfortable "gate area" seating. It follows the charming French custom of providing a piano for use by passengers waiting for their trains, albeit an upright rather a grand piano as in Gare de Lyon. We went into the Eric Kayser shop, bought a salad and some sandwiches, and sat down to eat. It dawned on us that we had found the perfect place to settle in for the next couple hours. Several other people were obviously doing the same thing. So we camped out there until it was time to board the train.

Our train was operated by a low-cost provider called OUIGO. Having heard that it was modeled on the bargain airlines, I was a bit apprehensive. But the train arrived right on time; the boarding process was very well managed (important, as the train stopped for only three minutes); and the coaches were essentially identical to the TGV coaches on the train from Paris to Avignon two weeks ago. It made a couple intermediate stops that made the ride about 20 minutes longer, but that was no problem. We used OUIGO only because all the TGV trains were booked solid, but it got the job done for half the cost.

We did have one close call. Toward the end of the run the train went below ground for a long stretch and eventually pulled into a large subterranean station. It seemed that everyone on the train was getting off so we figured this must be CDG. We let the other passengers go first and then muscled our luggage onto the platform. Suddenly Peggy said, "There are still some people on the train. I don't think this is the end of the line. I don't think it's the airport." I asked a guy walking by "Is this Charles DeGaulle?" His eyes widened and he said *"Oh, non, monsieur."* We immediately threw both our luggage and ourselves back into the coach just as the doors closed. I don't want to think about what a hassle it could have been had we gotten off at the wrong stop at the end of such a long day. Peggy really saved the day on that one.

About ten minutes later we pulled into the real CDG station. As with so many things in Paris, figuring out how to get from the station to our hotel was a bit bewildering. Fortunately we encountered English speakers at every turn to answer our question of the moment. It went like this: Wander up, down, and around the multi-storey station trying to find the free shuttle tram. Climb aboard the tram and try to remember which stop we were to take. Get off the tram only to find ourselves at a major parking structure in the middle of nowhere. Finally spy our hotel in the distance and set off on a ten-minute trudge under threatening skies, dragging our luggage behind us. I couldn't help but think of the scene in *Planes, Trains & Automobiles* in which Steve Martin does the same thing. "Bedraggled" was the word for how we looked and felt by this time.

But once we finally reached the hotel all went smoothly. We checked in, had a late buffet-style dinner, and conked out.

Heavy shutters to protect against the Mistral *wind*

TUESDAY, JUNE 4

Homeward Bound, Day 2

Things were blessedly straightforward today. Took an Uber to the airport terminal. Got through all the checkpoints very quickly, and so had a couple hours to relax in the duty-free area before boarding. I picked up a very nice bottle of Scotch that cost almost exactly the number of euros I had in my pocket that I wanted to get rid of (what were the odds?). The flight went very smoothly. I've been impressed by Air France's planes and service on this trip. I used to try to avoid them.

Our daughter Jane met us in the terminal in Detroit as we exited Customs (which, by the way, has really upped its game in terms of efficiency for the traveler). There's nothing quite as comforting as being welcomed by a familiar face at the end of a long journey.

Epilogue

I thought about The Man with the Baguette many times during our month in France. Where did he live? What did he do for a living? Did he have a family? Did he ever dream of spending a month in America?

A month was not enough time to get fully acquainted with him, or with what it really means to *live* in Paris or Provence. But we got more than a tourist's-eye view of both. We got in tune with the rhythms of daily life; with the routines of buying groceries, catching the bus, parking the car, even taking out the trash. In short: with being part of a neighborhood.

At one point I told Peggy that all I really need, and what I really want, is a gig with some person or company that needs the services of a vigorous retiree who can relocate to France for six months or so. Is that really too much to hope for?

www.ingramcontent.com/pod-product-compliance
Lightning Source LLC
Chambersburg PA
CBHW041228070526
44584CB00006B/325